✓ Are you ready to find out more about why you behave and communicate the way you do?

✓ Would you like to become a more effective communicator and more effective at accomplishing your goals?

✓ Do you want to understand why your coworkers, managers, subordinates, friends, and family members behave and communicate the way they do?

✓ Do you want to learn how to recognize and understand different personality and behavioral styles?

✓ Do you want to learn how to most effectively communicate with people of different personality and behavioral styles?

✓ Are you willing to invest some time to improve your communication and people skills?

✓ If you answered yes to any of the above, read on...

Communication-Skills
Magic

Improve Your Relationships &
Productivity through Better Understanding
Your Personality Style and the Personality
Styles of those Around You

E.G. Sebastian

www.egSebastian.com

www.iReadBodyLanguage.com

www.CommunicationSkillsMagic.com

Timshel Books · USA

Timshel Books Publishing

Copyright © 2010 - E.G. Sebastian

Timshel Publishing
Attn: E.G. Sebastian
330 Robert Smalls Pkwy, Ste 24
Beaufort, SC 29906
mailto:support@egSebastian.com

Ordering Information:
Order at www.CommunicationSkillsMagic.com or from the publisher at www.TimshelPublishing.com .

This book is available in paper-back format at **quantity discounts**. To get a volume quote, please view Appendix C at the end of the book; call TOLL FREE 877 379-3793, or visit us online at **www.CommunicationSkillsMagic/Volume_Discount.html**

ISBN #: 978-1-45051-334-0
Printed in the United States of America

Make your next event a smashing success!

Invite E.G. Sebastian to present a <u>keynote speech,</u>
or to present one – or several - of your <u>break-out sessions</u>:

- Improving Team Effectiveness
- Improving Managers' Effectiveness
- Conflict Management & Prevention
- How to Motivate Your Employees
- How to Deal with Difficult Customers
- How to Deal with Difficult Employees and Coworkers
- Improve Productivity through Improved Communication
- Improve Sales Performance through Understanding Your Sales Style and the Four Buying Styles
- How to Understand and Meet Your Customers' Needs

For more information,
contact E.G. toll FREE at 877 379-3793,
visit www.egSebastian.com
or by email at support@egSebastian.com

inscape publishing
Certified DiSC® Trainer

I dedicate this book to all my clients– past, present, and future clients –
who give me the privilege to impact their lives through
my workshops, keynotes, and personal coaching;

… and to my beautiful wife, Aida, who provides me
day after day with her unconditional love and support;
and my three children Alexa, Philip, and Adriana- who are the
joy of my life and are the best kids in the world
☺
Thanks guys for your support and for believing in me!

…

… and to Thomas Schlosser (1982 – 1997),
my youngest cousin; victim to
daily verbal and physical abuse;
who, in a desperate moment, decided
to end it all at the young age of 15.
If I forgot to say it while I had a chance,
I say it now: "I love you!"

Access your
FREE TRAINING VIDEOS

www.disc411.com

This is what you'll find here:
- Short history and intro to the DISC Behavioral Model concept
- Discover your personality style
- Explore your personality style's strengths and weaknesses
- Learn how to easily recognize different personality styles
- Learn HOW to connect effectively with people of different styles
- Discover the expectations each style has of you
- On-the-job behavioral tendencies of each style
- Explore ways to motivate different personality styles (great for managers and parents)
- How to deal with conflict with different styles
- Discover the ideal environment in which each style is most productive and feels most "at home"
- Challenge areas of the four styles (communication and task-completion)
- Explore effective ways to deal with the difficult people around you
- Explore how to connect most effectively with your clients
- Simple communication secrets to client retention
- Improve your productivity by capitalizing on your strengths and raising your awareness of your weaknesses
- and more... (new videos added monthly)

What others are saying about E.G.'s DISC-based programs?

This presentation brought me to the understanding how everyone is wired differently and to be aware of these differences. I learned to respect and better understand my coworkers.

Melissa Nelley - Communications Manager
DISC Presentation Participant

— — —

I don't want to say that your presentation was informational - it was rather TRANSFORMATIONAL. Now I have a more in-depth understanding of why my employees behave the way they behave, and I can clearly see that they have a better understanding of my communication and management style. It definitely changed the whole dynamics of the workplace.

Michael McCalvey - Chiropractor (and his team)
Improve Communication Skills through Understanding Behavior (DiSC) workshop participants, about 45 days after the event

— — —

A workshop that reminded all of us that everyone is motivated differently and helped us better understand different people with different personality types. E.G.'s style appeals to all types which encourages participation with everyone.

Carlotta Ungaro - President, Ch. of Commerce
DISC Presentation Participant

— — —

A presentation that I highly recommend for any group.

Liz Mitchel - Tourism Marketing Director
DISC Presentation Participant

Definitely a must-attend event for social workers. After this presentation I have a much better understanding of my clients' behavioral tendencies. Thank you for a very informative and entertaining presentation.

Danet Vernon - Social Worker
Improve Communication Skills through Understanding Behavior (DiSC) workshop participant

— — —

A wonderful session that helped me learn how to better manage and motivate my staff. Would I recommend this to others? Yes, Do it!

Hailey Orozco - Manager
DISC Presentation Participant

— — —

A great presentation that helped me understand how to better communicate with different types of personalities.

Ivey McClam - Membership Services Director,
DISC Presentation Participant

— — —

A wonderful learning experience! I enjoyed learning more about the people I work with and being more open and receptive to [individual] differences.

Catherine Hipp - Director of Tourism
DISC Presentation Participant

— — —

A very enjoyable presentation where I learned how to better interact with my coworkers.

Megan Krebs - Member Services Sales Associate
DISC Presentation Participant

I enjoyed discovering my personality type and finding out my coworkers personalities.

L.B. - Member Services Coordinator
DISC Presentation Participant

— — —

This session helped me better understand who I am, as well as better communicate and interact with my coworkers.

Jennifer Mead - Admin Assistant
DISC Presentation Participant

— — —

I learned to identify different personalities in children and adults, and learned how to most effectively communicate with each type. This is some information that I can apply immediately in my field.

Melissa Johnson - Different Personalities, Different Needs, Teachers' Mini-Conference participant

— — —

It helped me better understand myself and better understand my students, hopefully to make me a better teacher to each child.

Susan Hollister - *Different Personalities, Different Needs,* Teachers' Mini-Conference participant

Table of Contents

14

SELF-COACHING WORKSHEET I

How Committed Am I to Improving my Communication Skills?

Self-Coaching Worksheet I[1]

How Committed Am I to Improving my Communication Skills?

1. On a scale from 1 to 10, how committed are you to improve your communication skills?

| 1 | 2 | 3 | 4 | 5 | 6 | 7 | 8 | 9 | 10 |

Not
Committed
at All

Somewhat
Committed

Totally
Committed -
Nothing Can
Stop Me!

2. How would you benefit if you improved your communication skills and relationships with those around you?

At home _____

_____

At work _____

_____

Other_____

_____

_____

3. How would those around you benefit if you improved your communication skills?

_____

_____

_____

---

[1] - You can find a copy of this, and other assessments and worksheets online at **www.egsebastian.com/selfCoach**

4.   How much effort are you willing to put into improving this vital skill?

_____

5.   What could hinder you from developing into the communicator you know you could become?

_____

_____

_____

6.   What other resources do you need in order to succeed? (personal coaching, accountability partner, workshops, seminars, training   courses, counseling , anger management, develop self-esteem, etc)

_____

_____

_____

Action Steps / Notes:_____

_____

_____

_____

_____

_____

_____

_____

_____

Action Steps / Notes(continued): _____

_____

_____

_____

_____

_____

_____

_____

_____

_____

_____

_____

_____

_____

_____

_____

_____

_____

_____

_____

_____

_____

_____

_____

_____

_____

_____

Watch your thoughts; they become words. Watch your words; they become actions. Watch your actions; they become habits. Watch your habits; they become character. Watch your character; it becomes your destiny.

~ Author Unknown

Learning to understand and successfully manage diverse behaviors is a primary prerequisite to becoming effective at developing good communication skills and building lasting relationships.

This book was designed to help you recognize and better understand different behavioral styles – yours and of those around you - and will provide you a thorough guide to communicate more effectively with everyone in your environment based on understanding the needs of each individual.

Introduction

> Effective Communication – The Most Important Life-Skill
> How to Use this Book?
> Who Will Benefit from the Information in this Book?
> Why Can't We All Get Along Better?
> The Cost of Poor Communication & Conflict on Our Society
> Take an Honest Look in the Mirror
> Three Steps to Successful Relationships
> Not All Relationships are Created Equal
> Self-Assessment -How Successful Am I in My Relationships?
> You Can Easily Improve Your Communication Skills

Effective Communication – The Most Important Life-Skill

Let me ask you a question: How would it impact your life, at this very moment, if you could significantly improve your relationships with your coworkers, managers and/or subordinates, clients, parents, spouse, child(ren), and other significant people in your life?

> Creating better relationships through improving one's communication skills is most crucial to anyone's success, both in one's personal and professional life.

What if there was a system that could help you better understand your behavior and the behavior of those around you, and as a result improve your personal and/or professional relationships? Would it be worth the effort to give that system a try?

If you could improve your relationships dramatically, how much stress would be taken away from your days? How much more joy you'd get out of your time spent with your family and friends? How much more satisfaction you'd have at your workplace?

Creating better relationships, through improving one's communication and people skills, is not only possible for anyone who is wiling to put forth the necessary effort, but it is also undeniably the most crucial to any individual's success, both at home and at work.

In fact, I'd go so far to say that good communication and people skills are the most important skills one can acquire. There's no amount of organizational and technical skills that can make up for the lack of good communication skills both at home and at work (except, perhaps, in some highly technical or repetitive mechanical jobs where one can get by without communicating much with others).

Effective communication is an art - Period. And as with any art out there, we do not find too many people who truly master this art. Luckily, becoming an "artist" of effective communication does not require high IQ, advanced degrees, or any special talent. By learning the concepts laid out in the pages of this book you will undoubtedly be on your way to becoming a much better communicator.

> Good communication and people skills are the most important skills one can acquire. There's no amount of organizational and technical skills that can make up for the lack of good communication skills both at home and at work.

As Ralph Waldo Emerson said, "Every artist was first an amateur," and the same applies to effective communication: you have to start somewhere and through applying what you'll learn in the following pages you'll start seeing major positive changes on how you relate to people and how people start relating to you. Indeed, if you do take the time to apply the concepts in this book, your people skills – and hence your relationships – will "magically" rise to a level you only dreamt of accomplishing.

How to Use this Book?

This is not one of those books that you'd read in one sitting than throw it back on to the book shelf. If you choose to read the whole book in one sitting, that's great, but then come back and apply step by step what you read, especially the chapters that describe your style and the styles of the people you want to improve your relationships with.

You can also pick up the book as needed to read up on how to deal with a certain behavioral style in conflict, how to motivate that person, what are their strengths and weaknesses, hot to communicate most effectively with them, etc.

If you want to accelerate your learning and to take maximum advantage of the information laid out in the book, follow these steps:

1. Skip the intro chapter and go to page 66 (What is Your Behavioral Style?) to get a basic idea of what is your personality/behavioral style. In later chapters this information will help you understand why you get along better with some personality styles while people of certain personality styles tend to annoy you; as well as you'll find some specific suggestions that will help you become more productive, a better communicator, and more effective at building successful relationships.

2. Next, make sure to get a thorough - **really thorough!** - understanding of the information in Chapter 3 (especially the first sub-chapter titled *Most People's Behaviors are Highly Predictable*. Chapter 3 will help you discover how to recognize the 4 main behavioral styles (or personality styles). The rest of the book is in large part built on the information in Chapter 3.

3. Explore chapters 4, 5, 6, or 7 to learn about your behavioral style or the behavioral style of someone you want to improve your communication with.

4. Explore Chapter 8 to find out specific information on specific applications on any one of the four personality/behavioral styles (strengths, weaknesses, motivators, ideal environment, how to deal with each style in conflict, etc.).

Optional

5. Do you want to learn and apply the information laid out in the book most successfully?

   Teach it to others! Research has showed that when we take something that we just learned and we teach it to others, our learning improves dramatically.
   FREE handouts and basic PowerPoint slides available at **www.egSebastian.com/teach** -- please credit E.G. Sebastian and *Communication-Skills Magic* with the source of your information

---

To fully learn and anchor these concepts, teach them to others! You can find a FREE handout, basic PowerPoint slides, and instructions at **www.egSebastian.com/teach**[1].

Support your teaching with providing participants with a hard copy of this book. See volume discount prices in Appendix B, or online at **www.CommunicationSkillsMagic.com/volume**, or call 877 379-3793

If you would like to become a Certified DISC Trainer, view the information online at **www.egSebastian.com/certified,** **or call Toll Free 877 379-3793**

---

[1] - Please credit E.G. Sebastian's "Communication-Skills Magic" with the source of your handouts

Who Will Benefit From the Information in this Book?

When it comes to creating and maintaining successful relationships and effectively communicating with those around us, most of us dabble in the dark and communicate with others based on our instincts and past experiences; which sometimes works and at other times we end up frustrated with those around us and with ourselves.

This book provides some simple, yet powerful, information that will undoubtedly help you become a better communicator and improve your relationships with everyone around you. And the good news is that this is not a "band aid" method that will last for a short time, or one that works only with a few people around you. Throughout the book, you will be exposed to concepts and strategies that will help you become the successful communicator you always wanted to be.

No, these are not exaggerated statements – every year millions of individuals are exposed to these concepts[1] through company-sponsored training sessions, public seminars, tele-conferences, audio-products, books, articles, etc. The concepts laid out in the book are the same concepts taught to many Fortune 500 companies and to organizations of all sizes all over the world.

In the past more than three decades, more than 40 million people have been exposed to this information – this is probably the highest testimony to the popularity, effectiveness, and timelessness of these concepts.

The information outlined throughout the book will be useful for anyone who wants to improve their relationships, such as:
- Employees who understand that good communication skills are <u>at least</u> as important to a person's success as their technical skills
- Managers who want to: (1) improve their communication with employees, (2) learn to motivate each employee more effectively, and (3) want to understand what environments are most conducive to bringing out peak performance in each personality style
- Sales professionals who want to serve their clients more effectively and increase sales as a result of relating with more ease to prospective and existing clients

---

[1] -Known as The DISC Behavioral Model , The DISC Behavioral System, The Universal Language DISC, The Platinum Rule, etc., all of which are based on the concepts originally developed by psychologist William Moulton Marston, around 1927.

- Solo professionals who want to improve their relationships with their clients and have a desire to better understand their clients' motivators and needs
- Anyone who wants to improve their relationships with those around them (great for parents, spouses, etc.)

Managers and employees will benefit from understanding and applying the information in this book the following 7 ways:

1. Help managers better understand their employees' behavior, communication style, needs, and motivation
2. Help managers and employees better understand customers' and clients' needs, motivators, and communication style
3. Help employees get a better understanding of why their coworkers behave the way they do
4. Considerably reduce stress resulting from conflicts and personality clashes
5. Positively affect the bottom line by creating a customer and employee friendly environment
6. Gain new clients and keep existing ones with more ease due to a better understanding of their needs
7. Improve self-confidence due to improved communication skills and better understanding of self and others

For certain professionals it is crucial to have good people skills; have at least a basic understanding of human behavior and have great communication skills. For these professionals it is of outmost importance to be familiar with the information in this book. Some of these professions are:

- Managers
- Teachers
- Counselors
- Healthcare Professionals
- Social Services Providers
- Customer Service Reps
- Sales Professionals (Real Estate, Insurance, Financial Services, etc.)
- And anyone who works directly with people and need the ability to influence, motivate, or assist in a significant way

Organizations that put strong emphasis on providing this, or similar behavioral or personality style training, inevitably end up creating a workplace climate where everyone feels valued and understood, and where customers and clients feel that their needs are met and receive customer service beyond their expectations.

Why Can't We All Get Along Better?

Have you ever wondered why people around you behave the way they do? Did you ever wish that some of your family members, friends, or coworkers were a bit easier to communicate with? Have you ever found yourself wishing that some people around you were less difficult? Unless you are some relationship guru, it is more than likely that you have asked yourself these, or similar questions, regarding the behavior of the people around you.

Why are some people so hard to get along with? Why aren't we able to connect with everyone who we meet and maintain harmonious relationships? What causes the instant disconnect with some of the people around us? Is there anything that can be done that would help us improve our relationships with everyone around us – even with those who we perhaps perceive as difficult at the present moment?

These are the questions the chapters of this book will help answer.

The Cost of Poor Communication & Conflict on Our Society

Life can be really challenging when people around us don't get along and/or when we can't seem to be able to get along with others. Lack of good communication skills destroy families, poison workplace morale, and leads to lots of stress that could easily be avoided.

Undoubtedly communication skills are the most important skills one can acquire. Anyone who lacks good communication skills goes through life destined to encounter frequent conflicts and misunderstandings combined with an inability to maintain effective relationships in either personal or professional life.

> Undoubtedly communication skills are the most important skills one can acquire. Anyone who lacks good communication skills goes through life destined to encounter frequent conflicts and misunderstandings combined with an inability to maintain effective relationships in either personal or professional life.

Only through committing to a life-time of learning and growth in this area do we get to enjoy great personal and professional relationships and ultimately enjoy greater levels of success in all areas of our lives.

Studies have found that employees are often hired for their technical skills, but are often terminated for lack of good people and communication skills.

Unfortunately only few of us take studying communication skills seriously and our whole society suffers as a result:

- Workplace morale is often poisoned by coworkers who are poor communicators
- Lost productivity, high turnover, disciplinary actions, litigations are some of the other byproducts of on-the-job poor communication skills
- More than half of all marriages break up
- Many of the marriages and live-in relationships are filled with daily, or almost daily, arguments; what, sadly, is considered by many as a normal part of being in a relationship
- Many children grow up in hostile environments and often under regular verbal abuse (and neglect)
- Too many children grow up exposed to dysfunctional relationships, hence 1) they don't have a fair chance to develop good communication and social skills, and 2) are not exposed to positive role models that would help them grow into confident and well-balanced adults
- High stress levels produced by regular conflict, tension, and miscommunication, which often result in medical problems, such as ulcer, heart problems, etc.
- Of all medical visits, stress-related ailments account for billions of dollars spent every year

The above are only a few negative effects of poor communication on our society, but it should be enough to seriously inspire any one of us to spend more time developing our communication skills.

Take an Honest Look in the Mirror

Our everyday experiences are primarily dependent on two factors:

(1) Our ability to communicate effectively and

(2) Our ability to create successful relationships with those around us.

Without these two factors in place our journey on this planet can be quite challenging.

To find out if we have these two factors in place we have to be able to take an honest look in the mirror and ask ourselves:

- ☑ "Am I communicating effectively with those around me?"
- ☑ "Do I feel understood by most people in my environment?
- ☑ "Do I understand most people in my environment?"
- ☑ "Have I been able to develop and maintain successful relationships in my private life?
- ☑ "Have I been able to develop and maintain successful relationships in my professional environment?"
- ☑ "What areas of my interpersonal skills do I need to further polish in order to become more effective at creating and maintaining successful relationships in all areas of my life?"

Becoming aware of some of the areas that might need improvement, can be a great "first step" towards becoming a better communicator and better at building and maintaining successful relationships. Once you know what areas you need to improve upon, it is only a matter of getting the right information to make it happen.

This book will definitely provide you the tools to improve your communication and people skills in a matter of weeks, depending on how much time you are willing to dedicate to the process. By following the steps mentioned above, in the *How to Use this Book?* section, and by watching the training videos, you'll start seeing major positive changes in both your personal and professional relationships.

Three Steps to Successful Relationships

The information in this book will help you improve your communication skills – and ultimately help you improve your relationships – in three steps:

(1) get a good understanding of <u>why you behave the way you do</u>; hence raising your **self-acceptance** and **self-confidence** – both important prerequisites to becoming great at creating and maintaining successful relationships

(2) acquire a basic understanding of <u>why those around you behave as they do</u>; bringing about increased levels of acceptance of others, and

(3) learn how to communicate more effectively and create more successful relationships with individuals of different behavioral styles, including those "unreasonable," "difficult," "impossible," "crazy," and "non-cooperative" people in your environment, resulting in better relationships with everyone and reduced stress due to less conflict and fewer difficult relationships in your life

Does all this sound too complicated? If it does, do not let that discourage you. You will shortly see that the system described in this book – the DISC Behavioral System – is in fact really simple and common sense, yet this knowledge can have a tremendous impact on all of your personal and professional relationships.

The DISC Behavioral Model is a simple, easy to apply learning tool, yet the knowledge it provides can have a tremendous impact on all of your personal and professional relationships.

Not All Relationships are Created Equal

With most people around you it will most likely be enough to adopt some of the strategies laid out in the pages of this book and you will end up creating great, or greatly improved, relationships. Yet, when dealing with others, improved relationships will not be accomplished unless both parties get involved and work on it. (One way to accomplish that is by inviting the other person to a DISC Behavioral System based presentation[1], or give this book or a DISC based video as a gift to this person. See Appendix E for some more resources and get access to our constantly growing online database of **DISC AUDIO AND VIDEO CLIPS** (valued at $850.00+) by visiting **www.disc411.com**

One thing is sure: no matter where you stand in your relationships today, after going through the information in this book, your relationships with most people around you (and with yourself) will improve substantially.

---

[1] - To enquire about upcoming live seminars or teleseminars call TOLL FREE, 877 379-3793 or visit **www.egSebastian.com/events_calendar**

SELF-ASSESSMENT

How Successful am I in My Relationships?

Self-Assessment
How Successful am I in my Relationships?

Circle One:

1. On a scale from 1 to 10, how would you rate your ability to create and maintain successful relationships?

1	2	3	4	5	6	7	8	9	10

Somewhat   Somewhat   Extremely
Unsuccessful   Successful   Good

Check One:

2. I consider myself a good listener[1]

(While I listen... I keep good eye-contact; I don't get busy with other things; I don't display impatience by checking my watch, taping on the desk with my fingers, etc; I don't interrupt in the middle of sentences; my attention is focused on what is being said, not on what I'm going to say, or other non-topic-related ideas, etc)

_____   _____   _____
     Never   Sometimes   Usually

3. I find it easy to initiate meaningful conversations with family members and/or friends

_____   _____   _____
     Never   Sometimes   Usually

4. Communicating with my coworkers, managers, and/or subordinates is easy and comes naturally

_____   _____   _____
     Never   Sometimes   Usually

---

[1] - Assess and improve your listening skills with Inscape's Personal Learning Insights Profile® - **visit www.egSebastian.com/listening** for more info.

5. I think most people in my environment (family, friends, and/or coworkers) think of me as a good communicator

Never	Sometimes	Usually

6. When I sense that a conflict or argument is about to erupt, I have the ability to steer the conversation in a direction that will defuse the conflict/argument from surfacing.

Never	Sometimes	Usually

7. When (and if) I argue, I try to make sure that I listen well, making
sure that I first fully understand the other person's side.

Never	Sometimes	Usually

8. I believe that some people around me might come across as difficult due to a difference in our personality styles (Chapter 1)

Never	Sometimes	Usually

9. I am aware that most conflicts and misunderstandings happen due to my and others' (often unreasonable) behavioral expectations

Never	Sometimes	Usually

10. I believe that most people around me are basically good and want to get along with me and with one another

Never	Sometimes	Usually

11. I love to socialize with people who…
    a) … are humorous, dynamic, and extrovert
    b) … are more serious, focused, and formal
    c)… are soft-spoken, kind, and friendly
    d) … are fast-paced, determined, and outspoken
    e) … I successfully socialize with all of the above most of the time
    f) … I don't get along with most people around me

Scoring

For question **1**. rate your answer as follows:
o If you circled 1, 2, or 3 – give yourself **0 Points**
o If you circled 4, 5, or 6 – give yourself **1 Point**
o If you circled 7, 8, or 9 – give yourself **2 Points**
o If you circled 10, then look over the concepts in Chapter 2 then give the book as a gift to someone. You don't need it ☺

Question 1 ...._____

For questions **2**. through **8**., rate your answers as follows:
"Never - **0 Points**; "Sometimes" - **1 Points**; "Usually" - **2 Points**

Question 2 ...._____
Question 3 ...._____
Question 4 ...._____
Question 5 ...._____
Question 6 ...._____
Question 7 ...._____
Question 8 ...._____
Question 9 ...._____
Question 10.._____
For **Question 11.**, rate your answer as follows: ...._____
    If you circled **a)**, **b)**, **c)**, or **d)** – give yourself **1 Point**
    If you circled **e)**,   – give yourself **2 Point**
    If you circled **f)**,   – give yourself **0 Point**

Your Total   _____

Now check where your points fall:

15 to 22 Points
If your totals equal 15 or more, you should be rather proud of yourself. You either already spent some considerable time on developing your communication skills, or you got some good mentors or great upbringing; or perhaps you intuitively are adopting the right behaviors around people with different personality styles. Either way, you already have a good foundation on which you can continue building on. Surely you will find the concepts in the chapters ahead to greatly complement your already existing communication skills.

8 to 14 Points
If your totals equaled between 8 and 14 points, you probably get along well with some people, while with others it seems that there's some type of barrier in between the two of you. At times, you might even think that there might be something wrong with the other person (jerk, dumb, idiot, or other "creative" labels); or you might wander at times if there's something wrong with you.
This book will definitely be a great tool for you – you already posses some of the fundamentals of creating successful relationships. The info ahead might provide you with the missing link to transform you into the communicator you always wanted to become.

0 to 7 - Points
OK – you probably think that we live in a cruel world, where everyone is out there to get you. Or even worth, you might feel that you are not worthy enough to be out there and socialize with others. You probably spend lots of time in one of two extremes: 1) either arguing and/or being angry or 2) being hurt and withdrawn. If you have not committed yet to go through a complete communication skills makeover, the chances are that you'll stop reading this book before you'll finish Chapter 1. Hopefully, you got this book as part of your commitment to improving your communication skills and your relationships; in which case, Congratulations! Commit and follow through. This book will be an invaluable tool for you on your personal growth journey.

You Can Easily Improve Your Communication Skills

Yes, you can become a better communicator and create considerably more successful relationships if you are willing to put forth some effort, and equally importantly you commit to the process. Simply by reading this book already shows your commitment to improving your interpersonal skills.   Congratulations for that! ☺

Regardless of your score, this book will help you better understand those around you and will show you specific ways to deal with individuals who at this point might be perceived by you as difficult. After you'll start to apply what you learn throughout the following pages, you'll find that you will dramatically raise your ability to create and maintain successful relationships.

Commit to learning and applying the concepts in the following pages and you will undoubtedly go on creating better relationships with most people around you.

To better anchor your learning, go ahead and teach these concepts to others. You will find that these concepts are really simple and easy to remember, and the more you'll share it with others, the more you'll deepen your understanding of these concepts.

You can find FREE handouts and PowerPoint slides that you can use while sharing this info with others, at **www.egSebastian.com/teach**[1]   (On the same page you'll have access to more trainer resources.)

---

[1] - Please credit E.G. Sebastian's "Communication-Skills Magic" with the source of your handouts and PowerPoint.

The quality of your life
- both at work and at home -
is highly dependent on the quality of your relationships!

E.G. Sebastian

Chapter 1

Elements of Effective Communication
➢ The Definition of "Effective Communication"
➢ The #1 Key to Effective Communication
➢ Effective Communication Starts with Effective Listening
➢ Personality Style Theories
➢ The DISC Behavioral System
➢ Personality Style vs. Behavioral Style
➢ Most People Are Not Weird – They are Simply Differently Wired
➢ Power Tip #1: Commit to Listening at a Deeper Level

The Definition of "Effective Communication"

> *Effective communication is 1) the two way process – an exchange of ideas between two or more people - where all parties feel understood, respected, accepted, and are <u>comfortable to freely share ideas;</u> and 2) the ability to create and maintain harmonious relationships*
>
> *Effective communication does NOT (!) contain threats, name-calling, poking fun at the other person's expense, sarcasm, inducing shame or guilty feelings, or restricting the other person's <u>freedom of expression</u> – in one word, to communicate effectively one needs to <u>be aware of the other person's needs.</u>*

As you noticed in the highlighted info-box above, the concept of freely expressing one's ideas is stressed and underlined. "<u>Freedom to express oneself</u>" comes from the feeling of being understood and feeling respected enough to dare to speak out freely.

The #1 Key to Effective Communication

Effective communication cannot be accomplished unless one is aware of personality/behavioral style differences. A talkative, gregarious person expects most people around them to smile, talk openly about things, while also being considerate to others' feelings. An outspoken, bottom-line type person expects everyone to be brief and to the point, leave emotions out of the conversation, and be tough enough to take the honest and blunt truth. Put these two people to work in the same office and tensions and conflict will brew in a matter of days, unless at least one of them is aware of differences in behavioral

Through learning to understand different behavioral and personality styles, you will soon find that most people who you thought of as weird are simply differently wired and are 100% as "normal" as you or I.

or personality styles and knows how to talk the other personality styles "language."

Many of us have acquired some of this "wisdom" instinctively and through observation. We just learn about some people that "he's just like that" and we try to accommodate.

However, if we do take the time to truly understand why those around us behave the way they do, we'll all undoubtedly become more effective communicators and more successful at maintaining great relationships with everyone around us.

Effective Communication Starts with Effective Listening

Most effective communication courses put great emphasis on developing great verbal skills; however, only a few of those programs emphasize the crucial importance of good listening skills. Fact is, however, that without good listening skills, effective communication is not possible. And what only few people know, listening skills are learned – most of us are not born with it.

Steven Covey, in his book *Seven Habits of Highly Effective People*[1] stresses the importance of listening (Habit 5): *Seek first to understand, then to be understood.* Many of us get tangled up in trying to get our point across, while the other person tries the same, and all that's happening is two people speaking but NOT communicating.

So, yes, good communication skills start with good listening. Besides, let's face it, God/nature gave us two ears and only one mouth – shouldn't that be a clear message that we should listen twice as much as we speak?

Only by taking the conscious effort to <u>really listen</u> to those around us – and by observing some highly visible behavioral tendencies (that we'll cover in later chapters) – will ensure a good foundation to communicating effectively with loved ones, coworkers, or anyone with whom we decide that it's important to get along well.

What does the term *good listening skills* mean?

---

[1] - Steven Covey, Seven Habits of Highly Effective People. Simon and Schuster, New York 1989 (pg 239)

There are at least three levels of listening that we tend to adopt on a daily basis – which one describes your listening habits more closely?

Level 1 – While the other person speaks, I look at the person some of the time, I even nod my head at times in approval or disapproval, but most of the time I think about what I will answer (or even worse, I think about something totally unrelated to the topic). I regularly interrupt the other person; often with a totally unrelated topic.

Level 2 – While the other person talks, I keep good eye contact and listen to what the other person says, trying to really comprehend what I'm hearing. My mind does not wonder away to unrelated topics and my comments are directly related to the topic of discussion.

Level 3 – I listen to the other person with all my senses and I often "hear" even what is not expressed verbally. The person might tell me a fairly mundane story with a smile on her face, but I can sense if something is not right or if the person is bothered by something, depressed, or otherwise indisposed.

Of course, most of us tend to swing between the three levels, but each of us tends to spend more time listening at one level or another; unfortunately many of us tend to be stuck in Level 1 listening. Ideally, we should all strive to listen at level two, and occasionally at level three.

With a little effort – and conscious regular practice - anyone can learn to listen at level two:

- Keep good eye contact
- Listen intently to what the other person is saying
- Do not allow your mind to wonder away; consciously focus on the message that is being conveyed to you, trying to understand it (vs. thinking on what to reply to it)
- Ask questions related to the topic of discussion to help you understand better what is being said. This will also allow the other person see that you are really listening.
- Do not distract yourself (and the other person) with other tasks, such as shuffling papers, reading emails, jiggling your pocket change or your keys, playing with your hair, etc.
- Smile when appropriate

Most of us experience level three listening one time or another; however, most of us do not need to listen that deeply. This level of listening is mostly used by counselors, social workers, mental health workers (psychologists, psychiatrists, etc.), personal coaches, and other professionals. Parents also often experience this level of listening.

To be an effective communicator, take conscious effort to adopt the above bullet points to improve your **level two** listening. When you learn to listen well, your communication with those around you will improve significantly.

Good listening skills are a habit that can be developed. Combined with "reading" the behavioral or personality style of those around you, you'll become the great communicator you always wanted to be.

Personality Style Theories

For centuries there has been much research trying to better understand human behavior, and by today we have a plethora of assessments and systems that help us better understand ourselves and those around us. Of the many assessments and behavioral theories developed throughout times, the existence of four main temperaments, personality styles, or behavioral styles seemed to be one common element in most theories. Some of the most popular ones are described below:

Hippocrates' Bodily Fluids Theory

Around 400 B.C., Hippocrates, also known as "the father of medicine," developed the concept of temperaments. Unlike his predecessors who believed in the influence of the stars on human behavior, Hippocrates attributed one's temperament to a person's level of certain bodily fluids (or humors): blood, bill, black bill, and phlegm.

Hippocrates' bodily fluid theory became the basis of most research on personality, temperament, and behavioral types/styles.

Hippocrates identified four basic temperaments:
1. Choleric,
2. Phlegmatic,
3. Sanguine, and
4. Melancholy

Hippocrates' theory is still widely used; however, further research has showed that it was not the bodily fluids that caused people to have different temperaments, but rather one's genetic makeup and environmental factors. Years of research also improved the description of the four types.

Carl Jung's Psychological Types

In 1921, Dr. Carl Jung published his book *Psychological Types,* a book in which he described sixteen personality types, which he then categorizes into four main types:

1. the intuitor,
2. the thinker,
3. the feeler, and
4. the sensor.

The Myers-Briggs Type Indicator (MBTI)

The MBTI is based on Carl Yung's work - *Psychological Types, published in 1921* - and was developed in the 1940s by Katherine Cook Briggs and her daughter Isabel Briggs Myers.

It breaks down personality types into four broad dichotomies (groups of contradicting terms):

1. introversion/extroversion,
2. sensing/intuition,
3. thinking/feeling, and
4. judging/perceiving.

Depending on how the combination of these 4 dichotomies relate to a person, the MBTI groups people into 16 personality types

Keirsey Sorter

David Keirsey and Marylin Bates took the theories of Myers-Briggs and developed their own temperament sorter. In 1978 they published their findings in their book entitled *Please Understand Me* (Prometheus Nemesis Books).

The Bates' gave more user friendly names to the different types (vs. the multi-letter descriptors in the MBTI) and narrowed it down to 4 main temperament styles:

1. Artisan,
2. Guardian,
3. Rational, and
4. Idealist.

The Enneagram

The Enneagram thought to be introduced to the West (most likely coming from East) by the Russian George Ivanovitch Gurdieff. It was popularized in the United States by Don Richard Riso who further developed Gurdieff and others' work to develop a more complete and user friendly version.

Unlike most personality theories, the Enneagram divides personalities in nine types: 1. Reformer, 2. Helper, 3. Motivator, 4. Artist, 5. Thinker, 6. Skeptic, 7. Generalist, 8. Leader, and 9. Peacemaker.

The DISC Behavioral System

The DISC Behavioral Model was originally developed by William Moulton Marston in the 1920's, who published his findings in his book *The Emotions of Normal People,* in 1928. In the next decades, several researchers and companies have built on Marston's findings, till 1970 when John Geier and Dorothy Downey created the DISC Personal Profile System.

The DISC Personal Profile System – like most other personality theories - also identified 4 styles:

1. Dominance
2. Influence
3. Steadiness
4. Conscientiousness

In the next 30 years – following the creation of the DISC Personal Profile System – the DISC behavioral style profile (or DISC assessment, as some call it) was thoroughly researched and tested for validity and reliability and was continuously improved till the DISC based profile and DISC based seminars became one of the most popular behavioral-system-based learning tools on the market. By today more than 40 million[1] individuals worldwide have either completed a DISC profile[2] or have participated in a DISC seminar.

A highly distinguishing characteristic of the DISC Behavioral System is that it helps individuals go beyond better understanding themselves, build more successful relationships, and improve performance – all extremely helpful characteristics; however, the DISC Behavioral System also helps in easily recognizing different behavioral styles that one encounters on a daily basis and provides simple and easy-to-remember guidance on how to most effectively communicate with each style.

> A highly distinguishing characteristic of the DISC Behavioral System is that it helps you recognize individuals of different behavioral styles around you, and provides simple and easy-to-remember guidance on how to most effectively communicate with each style.

This additional element of helping me (the author) understand those around me was what made me fall in love with DISC. As I sat through my first 4-hours DISC seminar, it felt as if someone had turned the light on in the realm of my relationships. Suddenly I understood sooo many things about myself and others – things that bugged me since I was in elementary school. "Why did I see humor (fun) in everything?" "Why was I so outgoing and getting into so much trouble" "How come other kids were able to be so conscientious and obedient, while I was always impulsive and disobedient?" - all questions that stayed with me till adulthood.

With the understanding I gained in that first DISC seminar came a level of acceptance

… my attempt to understand those around me was limited by my biased perception of "right" and "wrong" as seen through the lens of my personality and behavioral style.

---

[1] - Based on Inscape Publishing, Inc. research

[2] - You can complete the DiSC® Classic Profile and view a brief description of it - and a sample profile - online at **www.egsebastian.com/disc_classic**

of myself and the diverse people with different behavioral styles around me; acceptance that I have not experienced prior to that event. Suddenly I realized that for years my attempt to understand those around me was limited by my biased perception of "right" and "wrong" as seen through the lens of my personality and behavioral style. Suddenly I understood family members, friends and coworkers who for years I labeled as "pushy," "airhead," "softy," "nitpicky," and other labels that wouldn't look very pretty in print. This new understanding – especially of my close family members - was worth to me more than if I had won the jackpot on the lottery.

After that first fateful event I became a much better father and husband: more understanding and patient when facing behavioral and communication differences that I now embraced in those that I love. Interacting with my business clients took on a totally different form as well, treating now everyone as <u>they wanted to be treated</u> - based on my understanding of each individual client's behavioral style[1].

But before I get carried away and write 6 pages on how DISC has changed my relationships with family members, friends, and clients, it's enough to say that I was so much affected by that first DISC seminar that I decided to learn everything I could about it, get trained, go to school, get certified – whatever it took – and get out there and affect others' lives, the same way as mine was affected.

That is how I became a full-time DISC facilitator, trainer, and consultant, and that is why this book is based on the DISC behavioral system. I believe the DISC behavioral system is the best tool for helping anyone better understand human behavior – both one's own behavior and the behavior of others. Read the book carefully – and do participate in a live DISC seminar[2] if you have a chance – and see how it will positively affect your relationships with everyone around you.

---

[1] - Most individual clients are given a DiSC® PPSS* assessment at the beginning of our business or coaching relationship, which proves extremely helpful for both of us; the knowledge gained this way empowers me to treat the client as she or he wants to be treated. This tool also helps me – as a coach and consultant – to get an understanding of the client's risk taking tolerance, fears, motivators, strengths, weaknesses, etc. See a more detailed description of the DiSC PPSS at **www.egsebastian.com/disc_ppss**

* DiSC is a registered trademark of Inscape Publishing, Inc.

[2] - To enquire about upcoming live seminars or teleseminars call TOLL FREE, 877 379-3793 or visit **www.egSebastian.com/events_calendar**

Personality Style vs. Behavioral Style

Personality Style = refers to a person's *relatively* <u>*stable*</u> *psychological and behavioral characteristics - the way the person views the world and relates to it. Personality remains, more or less, the same across various situations*[1].

Behavioral Style = the set of behaviors one tends to adopt on a consistent basis.
<u>It does not measure, nor is dependent, on one's intelligence, IQ, education level, or mental health.</u>

For many of us there's probably not one day passing by without hearing the word "personality." We hear it at home or at work when speaking about someone: "She has a cheerful personality," "He is sooo boring – he has no personality at all," and other similar comments. Fact is, of course, that each one of us has personality, and we all have different personalities.

When it comes to personality, there has been a debate for years that scientists do not seem to be able to come to terms with; regarding whether personality is something that is genetically imprinted in us or is it something that's shaped by the environment. The truth probably lies in between the two extremes: we are born with a certain genetic predisposition towards a certain personality style, but our personalities are also greatly shaped by our environment.

Maternity nurses who studied personality or behavioral styles say that they recognize a child's styles a few hours after birth. Parents of multiple children also know that each child can be extremely different from one another right from the first day; and as a parent of three children, I can attest to that. So, yes, all evidence shows that we are born with different personality styles, but then that style is shaped by the environment as one goes through stages of life.

---

[1] - Martin E.P. Seligman et. Al., Abnormal Psychology. W.W. Norton & Company, Inc., pg 371

Can one's personality or behavioral style change? This is a question that regularly comes up in my DISC-based presentations and workshops. As I describe the four main DISC styles, people occasionally perceive one style as more favorable then the others, and they wish they could change their style to mirror the one they like.

No, we cannot change our personality style. Much of it, as I mentioned above, is determined by our genetic makeup and there's nothing we can do about that. The good news is that each of the four main styles has its distinct set of strengths, as well as weaknesses, and by capitalizing on our strengths we can each become more productive; and by understanding our style's weaknesses, we can take steps to improve in those areas.

While we cannot change our personality style, what we can control, however, is our behavior. Regardless of our personality style, we can choose to adopt behaviors that are most effective in different situations, and through awareness or our strengths and weaknesses and self-control we can choose to eliminate or redirect behaviors that don't serve us in creating the relationships we want to create with those around us or hinder us in our productivity and attainment of our goals.

Our personalities are expressed through our behaviors, but unlike personality style – which is more or less stable - our behaviors are adaptable. In the pages of this book we'll talk about "behavioral styles," which are also rather stable; but once one becomes aware of his or her behavioral style, the individual has more control over it and can choose to adopt more effective behaviors in order to better connect and communicate with people of different personality/behavioral styles.

In the later chapters you'll discover the four main behavioral styles and you'll learn that it is up to you to adopt behaviors from any of the four styles in order to get along and communicate most effectively with everyone around you.

> You've encountered in your reading so far the terms "personality style" and "behavioral style"; since the information in this book is based on the DISC Behavioral System, we'll go on using throughout the book the term *behavioral style.*

Most People Are Not Weird – They are Simply Differently Wired

In some of our interactions with others – at times, even when we meet total strangers - we feel connected instantly; we seem to hit it off and chat right away about all kinds of personal, political, or just trivial topics. On the other hand, there are those individuals who we meet, work with, or otherwise get in touch regularly, and not even years of interacting with them can create any type of sense of connectedness to them. We just can't seem to be able to relate to them, or even worse, we are annoyed by some of these people each time we meet them. And, of course, most people we meet are somewhere in between these two extremes.

> There are two sides to every coin. Is it possible that the people we see as behaving inappropriately might view us as the ones who behave out of sync?

In a society where we encourage and celebrate freedom of speech and promote respect for individual differences, it is only normal that we face almost on a daily basis behaviors that at times may seem – to say the least – odd; or even inappropriate, annoying, and stressful. But let's face it, there are two sides to every coin. Is it possible that the people we see as behaving inappropriately might view us as the ones who behave out of sync?

Through learning to understand different behavioral and personality styles you will soon find that most people who you thought of as weird are simply differently wired – have a different personality style from yours - and are 100% as "normal" as you or I.

Who is right and who is wrong? Is it possible that neither is right or wrong?

Fact is, we get along best with people who have similar behavioral (or personality) styles as ours, and we often view those who have different personality styles as "weirdoes," "strange," and other creative labels.

Can we do anything to change the behavior of our coworkers, customers, family members, or friends who might come across at times as unreasonable, non-cooperative, argumentative, or otherwise difficult? Most likely not; but we can definitely <u>learn to better understand their behaviors</u> and communicate more effectively with each individual based on that understanding. Learning to understand different behavioral styles also greatly affects our perception of those around us; it will help us see people as "different," not "difficult."

Power Tip #1
Commit to listening at a deeper level to those around you

We all like people who listen to us; none of us like poor listeners and those who interrupt us constantly.

Improve your relationships by listening more carefully to those around you and try to empathize – listen more carefully and take a conscious effort to understand the other person's side "of the story."

Real listening skills are expressed through
> keeping good eye contact
> asking questions related to the topic
> not interrupting – especially not with an unrelated topic or idea (a true "deadly sin" and a hallmark of ineffective listeners)
> listening to what is being said, vs. getting lost in thoughts the conversation brings up, or other non-topic related thoughts;
> nod occasionally (constant nodding is perceived as annoying by most people)
> do not perform tasks while listening (typing, numbers-crunching, looking for something, etc.)

NOTES: _____

Chapter 2

An Introduction to the DISC Behavioral System

➢ Follow The ~~Golden~~ People-Smart Rule!

➢ The Basics of the DISC Behavioral System

➢ This System Works!

➢ The Journey Starts with Understanding Yourself

➢ What is Your Behavioral Style?

➢ Power Tip #2: Focus on the Strengths of Those Around You

Follow The ~~Golden~~ People-Smart Rule!

> **Warning!!! When it comes to communicating with others, applying The Golden Rule can be extremely counterproductive!**

We've been taught ever since childhood to follow The Golden Rule "Do unto others as you would have them do unto you," but when it comes to *effective communication,* The Golden Rule can be straight out counterproductive and can result in conflict and constant tension with certain people around you. What we all need to realize is that not everybody wants to be treated the same way as each of us do.

Steven Covey, in his book *7 Habits of Highly Effective People[1],* says that the Golden Rule should be rather understood as "Understand [others] deeply as individuals, the way you would want to be understood, and then treat them in the terms of that understanding." This gives the golden rule a quite significant tweak, and we'll call this rule "The People-Smart Rule," which put in simpler language would sound something like, *Respect others by treating them as THEY want to be treated* (vs. treating them as YOU would want to be treated).

The Golden Rule is basically about *"respect"* – respect others by doing to them what you don't mind being done *unto* you – and what better way is to show your respect to those around you than by trying to understand how they want to be treated and treat them accordingly.

> You need to realize that most people do not want to be treated the way you want to be treated.

Just think about it for a moment…

We all know people who are very private and totally dislike "nosy" questions, while others not only don't mind, but welcome any types of questions (introvert vs. extrovert). Now, should the extrovert person treat everyone as she would like to be treated? (Or vice-versa?) We all know that's rarely a good way to build great relationships.

---

[1] - Steven Covey, Seven Habits of Highly Effective People. Simon and Schuster, New York, 1989 (pg. 192)

To become effective communicators, we need to learn to recognize the behavioral styles of those around us and treat them as they want to be treated

---

The People-Smart Rule:

*Respect others by treating them as **THEY** want to be treated*

(vs. treating them as YOU want to be treated)

When we apply The Golden Rule, we treat others through the assumption that "This is how I want to be treated, and that's how I'll treat you too." The *People-Smart Rule,* on the other hand, teaches to first try to understand how those around you want to be treated, and treat them accordingly.

How would one do that? You might ask…

This book, through introducing you to the DISC Behavioral System, will provide the necessary guidance on helping you easily recognize the different behavioral styles around you, understand each style's needs, and you'll be introduced to concrete strategies on how to effectively communicate with each individual based on that understanding. That is, you will learn to treat everyone the way they want to be treated.

The Basics of the DISC Behavioral System

Have you ever wondered why some people around you are always on the go, upbeat, and seem to have no fear of anything, while others seem to be more withdrawn, controlled, and often worry about all kinds of "trivial" things?

Have you wondered why YOU behave the way you do?

Human behavior is very complex and we are all very unique, but you'll be surprised to learn how predictable each of us is in more ways than you have ever imagined.

The good news is that, with a little effort, anyone can learn to recognize and understand

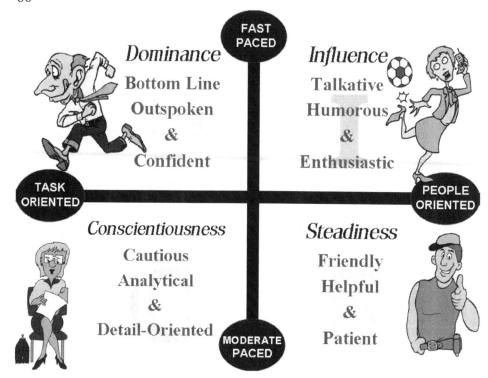

Figure 2.1 – DISC describes behavior in four styles: Dominance, Influence, Steadiness, and Conscientiousness[1]

different behavioral styles, simply by noticing a few externally observable behaviors, and have an instant understanding of a person's communication and behavioral tendencies. Then armed with that knowledge, it's only a matter of applying what you'll learn in this book to build better, more successful relationship with anyone around you.

The DISC Behavioral Model (See Fig. 2.1) is a learning tool that will help you better understand why you behave as you do, why those around you behave as they do, will help you better manage your expectations of those

You will learn to recognize the 4 main DISC behavioral styles around you, understand each style's needs, and you'll be introduced to concrete strategies on how to treat everyone the way THEY want to be treated.

---

[1] - The terms "Dominance, Influence, Conscientiousness, and Steadiness" are terms originally used by Inscape Publishing, Inc

around you, and through this knowledge you will be empowered to create better relationships with mostly anyone around you.

DISC explores behavior across four styles: 1. Dominance (D), 2. Influence (I), 3. Steadiness (S), and 4. Conscientiousness (C); hence the acronym DISC. Each style – D, I, S, and C – is described through a set of behaviors that enables us to explore and better understand the behavioral styles and the combination of styles of the individuals we encounter in our everyday interactions.

A person would be considered to be D, I, S, or C style, based on the person's natural tendency to adopt behaviors from a particular style's set of behaviors. For example, if someone tends to adopt mostly behaviors from the Steadiness set of behaviors, we would call this person a Steadiness style (or S style) person. Or if someone seems to consistently display behaviors from both the Conscientiousness and the Dominance set of behaviors, we'd call this person a DC or CD style individual. We will get into more details on this a little later in this chapter, and more in depth in, Chapters 4, 5, 6, and 7.

A distinctive characteristic of the DISC Behavioral Model - as compared to other personality and behavioral theories - is the simplicity of the four-quadrant model that allows anyone to easily recognize the behavioral styles of the individuals around us (see Fig. 2.1 on previous page). This understanding of the styles often results in increased acceptance of individuals with diverse behaviors, enables one to communicate more effectively with each style, while also aiding in understanding each style's

- motivators
- demotivators
- strengths
- fears
- possible weaknesses
- communication style
- expectations of others
- possible conflict triggers
- compatibility with individuals of each style
- and other behavioral tendencies (explored in more details in Chapters 4, 5, 6, and 7; as well as in Chapter 9).

> **It is important to understand that one's personality style does not predetermine someone to being "good" or "bad"** – it is a person's belief's and values that will ultimately influence a person's actions and tendency to do good or bad.

This System Works!

More than 40 million[1] people worldwide have used Inscape Publishing DiSC®[2] profiles to help them better understand themselves, better understand others, and to improve their relationships.

The DISC model has been used in the past three decades by everyday people from all walks of life, as well as companies of all sizes (including Fortune 500 companies) to help employees:

- explore their behavior and the behavior of those around them in a safe and non-judgmental manner
- improve communication skills
- reduce workplace conflict
- increase acceptance of diverse behaviors
- improve productivity
- improve team effectiveness
- improve team spirit
- and more…

While most popular personality and behavioral systems on the market are great at helping understand a person's own behavior, there are only a very few that help understand others' behaviors as well. And that's one of the attraction factor and benefit that the DISC Behavioral Model provides.

By learning to recognize and understand the different behavioral styles of those around us, coupled with understanding each style's behavioral and communication tendencies can be extremely useful in most areas of our lives, such as…

---

[1] - Based on Inscape Publishing, Inc. data. Inscape Publishing is the leading provider of DiSC® and other learning instruments, providing learning tools in 25 languages in more than 50 countries (**www.InscapePublishing.com**)

[2] DiSC® - with lower case "i" is an Inscape Publishing , Inc trademark

On the Job:
- managers can better manage and motivate their subordinates due to better understanding employees' needs, motivators, fears, strengths, possible weaknesses, and other general behavioral tendencies
- improve communication with coworkers
- reduce conflict, hence more time is spent productively
- improve team spirit
- improved productivity due to better employee relationships and less time spent on conflict, misunderstandings, etc.
- improved employee retention due to creating a better workplace environment

In Coaching Applications to help clients or employees
- understand their strengths and weaknesses
- capitalize on their strengths
- became aware of, and work on, weaknesses
- become more effective at completing tasks and accomplishing goals
- raise awareness of how to effectively sell to different styles (for sales professionals)
- deal more effectively with conflict
- avoid conflict

In Romantic Relationships:
- increased understanding and acceptance of the other person
- reduced conflict
- improved communication

For Parents:
- increased understanding and acceptance of the child's behavior
- easier parenting due to a better understanding of the child's needs, motivators, and natural drive
- reduced conflict
- improved communication

These are only some of the top applications. This system is applied in many other areas as well, such as improving relationships with:
- siblings,
- parents,
- in schools to improve teachers' understanding of their students (and improve communication with other staff members),

- nurses, to better understand their patients (and improve communication with other hospital employees),
- for clergy, to better understand their members,
- and a myriad more areas

The Journey Starts with Understanding Yourself

"Know yourself" - Socrates (Circa 470–399 BC)

Understanding others' behaviors was a pursuit of mankind since the beginning of civilization and we still continue pursuing this quest of trying to understand the intricacies of the human mind and the behaviors it orchestrates. Let's face it, life would be so much easier if we were able to better understand the behaviors of those around us.

But, before we discuss others' behaviors, let's explore a little closer to home:

☑ Do you know why YOU behave as you do?

☑ Have you got any idea why you approach and pursue your tasks and goals as you do vs. how others do it?

☑ Do you notice yourself when you are being difficult once in a while?

☑ Do you understand why you are being difficult at those times?

☑ Do you have any idea why some perceive you as a great person while others just don't seem to appreciate you?

Understanding the answers to these questions will undoubtedly lead to improving your relationships and ultimately your whole life[1].

Sun Tsu (circa 544 -496 AD) in his timeless military strategy book "The Art of War[2]" said: *So it is said that if you know your enemies and know yourself, you will not be imperiled in a hundred battles; if you do not know your enemies but do know yourself, you will win one and lose one; if you do not know your enemies nor yourself, you will be imperiled in every single battle.*

---

[1] - One of the benefits of becoming familiar with the DISC Behavioral System is its coverage of each style's effectiveness in initiating and completing tasks and goals, which often determines one's success on the job and private life.

[2] - Sun Tzu, The Art of War. Shambhala, 2005

Sun Tsu's teachings on the value of knowing one's enemy and self are entirely transferable to our relationships. And while we (hopefully) can't call the other party in any of our relationships "enemy," they can easily turn into something similar to an enemy if we don't have a basic understanding of why we do what we do and why the other person behaves as he or she does.

Hence, Sun Tsu's teaching translated into "relationship language" would be: *if you understand the behavior of those around you and understand your own behavior, you will avoid hundreds of conflicts; if you do not understand others but do know yourself, you will avoid some conflict and get drawn into some; if you do not understand others' behaviors nor yours, you are doomed to spend most of your life in conflict and miscommunication.*

Many participants in my seminars say that (one of) the greatest benefit they get from participating in my DISC presentation was primarily the better understanding of themselves – the realization that "it is OK to be who I am – I am "normal," and this realization leads to a great sense of self-acceptance. In many cases, this self-acceptance results in instant higher confidence levels due to understanding that there's "nothing wrong with me – I am not broken." Participants become more aware of their strengths and learn how they can better capitalize on them; as well as they get to face some of their weaknesses and learn to better accept them or use this new knowledge to work towards improving some weaker areas.

So, let's get started and find out, first of all, what is YOUR behavioral style; which, in turn, will help you get a better understanding of your behavioral tendencies and communication style.

Take a few minutes and explore the

What would Sun Tzu say?

If you understand the behavior of those around you and understand your own behavior, you will avoid hundreds of conflicts; if you do not understand others but do know yourself, you will avoid some conflict and get drawn into some; if you do not understand others' behaviors nor yours, you are doomed to spend most of your life in conflict and miscommunication.

next sub-chapter entitled *"What is Your Behavioral Style [1]?"* to get an idea of what is YOUR style. This way, as you read on, you'll be able to focus your attention on parts of the book that will help you better understand the behavioral style that you might adopt more naturally and start exploring ways on how to improve your communication skills and productivity.

What is Your Behavioral Style?

Take a few minutes now to review a brief description of the four styles, and check the one that you feel describes you most closely.

_____ **Dominance (D) Style** (*Fast Paced/Task Oriented*)

High[2] D style individuals are characterized by fast pace, fast rate of speech, a strong desire of being in charge, and are highly focused on accomplishing goals and completing tasks. On the job, they are the ones who lead by example, while also will push everyone to perform and leave little room for personal chit-chat. They know what they want, they go for it, and they expect those around them to do the same. D style individuals are goal-oriented, process driven, and often turn out to become real achievers. At times, due to their drive to accomplish goals and their high focus to complete the tasks they work on, they are perceived as cold, pushy, inpatient, and as having little consideration for the feelings of those around them.

D's try to avoid, whenever possible, routine work, and environments where they are not given the freedom to be in charge (at least) of their own actions, and are not allowed to move at their own (fast) pace. (See a more detailed description of the D – Dominance Style - in Chapter 4)

---

[1] - To take the validated and reliable DiSC® (2.0 or PPSS) assessment, please visit **www.egsebastian.com/assessments**

[2] - These are general tendencies of individuals who scored "sky" high on one of Inscape's DiSC® assessments, such as the DiSC 2.0 or the DiSC PPSS

_____ **Influence (I) Style** *(Fast Paced/People Oriented)*

High I style individuals are characterized by fast pace - both in actions and speech – and a love to socialize. I style individuals are easily recognized by their high energy levels, enthusiasm, and their openness to interaction with others at any moment of the day. They tend to almost constantly smile and be ready to share a joke, a (humorous) story, or listen to others' stories (even though, listening is not their main strength – they rather talk than listen). They come across as friendly, enthusiastic, and passionate; and at times can be perceived as fake (too much smiling and enthusiasm) and tiring (too much talking).

I's style individuals dislike environments where they are not given the freedom to interact with others, have to perform routine and detail-oriented activities, or are not given a chance for quick and regular recognition. (See a more detailed description of the I – Influence Style - in Chapter 5)

_____ **Steadiness (S) Style** *(Moderate Paced/People Oriented)*

High S style individuals are characterized by being moderate paced - both in speech rate and physical movement – and by a strong tendency to support others. S style individuals enjoy being around people, and due to their tendency of being more thoughtful and caring, they are great listeners and come across as friendly and warm. S style people are calm, amiable, and supportive. They are perceived by many to be the sweetest people in the world and most of us enjoy having them around us. Due to their calm, cautious, and hesitant nature, at times they can come across as being a bit slow at performing certain tasks and slow at making decisions.

S style individuals will often try to avoid fast-paced environments with unpredictable work schedules, and will stay away as much as possible from any situations where they would have to put up with regular conflict or otherwise stressful situations.. (See a more detailed description of the S – Steadiness Style - in Chapter 6)

_____ Conscientiousness (C) Style *(Moderate Paced/Task Oriented)*

High C Style individuals are characterized by being cautious, moderate paced, and highly task oriented. C style individuals enjoy working individually or with a small group of other C style individuals. They like getting deeply involved in performing tasks and do not like to be interrupted while working. They tend to be very particular about doing an excellent job and are very organized. Due to their natural tendency to be analytical and questioning, C style individuals are great in any area where accuracy and precision is needed. To the other three styles, C style individuals can at times come across as distant, perfectionist, and overly nit-picky.

C style individuals will try to avoid fast-paced environments where they'd have to make quick decisions, spend most of their time on social niceties, and where they would have no time to plan carefully their days. (See a more detailed description of the C – Conscientiousness Style - in Chapter 7)

Remember! No one is purely one style or another; we are all a combination of two or more of the styles described above.

Important!

The DISC Behavioral Model does not suggest that we are stuck in one behavioral style or another (!). It is designed to raise awareness of our behavioral tendencies; then use this knowledge to take control – or gain acceptance – of our weaknesses and limitations, while focusing on capitalizing on our strengths.

Power Tip #2

Focus on the strengths of those around you!

Improve your relationships by noticing the strengths of those around you and by showing your appreciation for those strengths; especially try to notice the strengths of those people who in the past you might have only noticed their weaknesses.

Understand that often the people whom you might dislike most (perhaps due to their personality style that's opposite to yours) possess strengths that best complement your weaknesses. In a business environment often these people are the ones who you need most in order to be most effective.

Chapter 3

The DISC Behavioral Model

> Most People's Behaviors are Highly Predictable
> Understanding Your Behavioral Style
> Understanding Others' Behavioral Styles
> Common Characteristics of the Four Behavioral Styles
> Common Characteristics: A Humorous Look ☺
> Funny and Practical "Facts" - Fast Pace vs. Moderate Paced individuals
> Funny and Practical "Facts" - Task Oriented vs. People Oriented
> How to Recognize Different Behavioral Styles
> General Tendencies of the Four DISC Styles
> DISC Statistics
> You Are in Charge of Your Behavior
> Power Tip #3: Avoid Judging Others…

Most People's Behaviors Are Highly Predictable

Our day to day life experiences are greatly shaped by our perception of the world, our behaviors, and perception of those around us – and therefore how we relate to people and events. But we also posses certain traits that we are born with that contribute to a great extent to shaping our personalities and behaviors, and hence determine to a high degree how we relate to the world (and people) around us. Due to this mix, we are all unique beings creating a colorful world of diverse behaviors

While it is a fact that we humans are extremely complex beings, displaying infinitely diverse behaviors, it might surprise you to see that based on some observable behavioral clues, how very much predictable many of our behaviors tend to be.

We have known at least since Hippocrates (circa 400 BC) that there were <u>four main behavioral styles</u> (or *temperaments,* as Hippocrates called them) and those findings were supported by modern research as well (though his original theory of bodily fluids influencing one's temperament was discredited). The four styles are rather easy to recognize once one learns what clues to look for.

The clues to one's behavioral style are few and simple. Research[1] has shown that we tend to display a specific set of behaviors based on two factors (or clues):

(1) a person's pace and
(2) a person's people vs. task orientation. (See Fig. 3.1)

Important!
The DISC Behavioral Model does not suggest that we are stuck in one behavioral style or another (!). It is designed to raise awareness of our behavioral tendencies; then use this knowledge to take control – or gain acceptance – of our weaknesses and limitations, while focusing on capitalizing on our strengths.

---

[1] - The DISC Behavioral Model is based on William Moulton Marston's research. Inscape Publishing, Inc built on Marston's findings.... Request a copy of the research conducted by Inscape Publishing, Inc., by sending an email to support@egSebastian.com

Clue #1: Pace

Does this person usually move and talk at a faster pace **OR** more moderate pace?

> Some of us tend to be more
> 1) outgoing: speak fast, move fast, bring quick decisions; while others tend to be more
> 2) reserved: move and talk at a more moderate pace, as well as take their time to think through all variables before bringing a decision.

Obviously, it is easy to recognize those who display behaviors from either of these two extremes; many individuals, however, are somewhere on the continuum in between the two extremes.

Clue #2: Task vs. People Orientation

Does this person a) usually enjoy socializing, **OR** b) usually prefers working on task-oriented activities (or talk about task-oriented topics)

> **a)** Some love to be most of the time around people, love to socialize, and like to work in environments where they can spend considerable time working with people (nurses, social workers, teachers, actors[1], etc)
>
> **b)** while others prefer to spend most of their time working on tasks, building something, doing research, working with concepts, and other task-oriented activities (engineers, pharmacists, accountants, pilots, etc.)

Again, it is easy to recognize those who display behaviors from either of these extremes; you will find, however, that most individuals are somewhere on the continuum in between the two extremes.

---

[1] - See a list of careers preferred by each behavioral style at the end of Chapter 4, 5, 6, and 7.

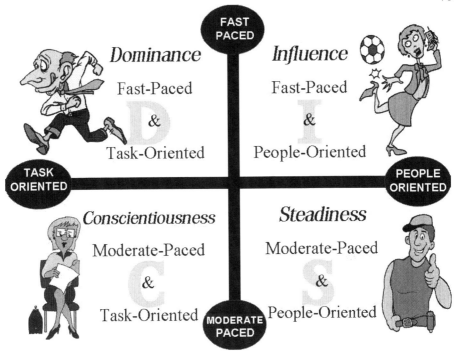

Figure 3.1 – Pace and People vs. Task Orientation

As you probably noticed, I repeated the "clues" to one's behavioral style several times in the previous pages, and I'll go over them a few more times in the next few pages, and with good reason. Repetition is the mother of learning, right? Besides, I want you to remember to watch for these clues when interacting with those around you. **Remembering these clues is the first step to identifying, understanding, and ultimately improving your communication with the individuals with different behavioral styles in your environment.** As you read on you will learn that these two factors (pace and task vs. people orientation) greatly determine an individual's behavioral style and the behaviors one tends to display consistently.

While it is a fact that we humans are extremely complex beings, it might surprise you to see that based on some observable behavioral clues, how very much predictable many of our behaviors tend to be.

Based on pace and orientation, the DISC Behavioral System will help you explore human behavior in four main styles: (See Fig. 3.1 on pg. 73)

Dominance (D) – *fast paced* and *task oriented*
Outspoken and determined, D's are dynamic, goal-oriented people who like to take charge, bring quick decisions, and want quick results

Influence (I) – *fast paced* and *people oriented*
Enthusiastic and friendly, I's are outgoing, high-energy people who like to influence others with their wit, humor, and persuasive skills

Steadiness (S) – *moderate paced* and *people oriented*
Caring and supportive, S's are calm and kind people, who are great at providing support and comfort to others, follow rules, are great listeners and great team players.

Conscientiousness (C) - *moderate paced* and *task oriented*
Cautious and detail-oriented, C's are focused and dependable people who love to work with tasks and concepts; like to plan their work and are committed to quality and accuracy in all areas.

Once you recognize the dominant style of another person, you can easily predict a whole set of behaviors of that person, as well as better understand WHY that person behaves as she does. This information allows the person familiar with the DISC system to better understand why someone behaves the way she does and improve communication based on that understanding.

> A person's **dominant** *behavioral style* is determined by one's tendency to display behaviors from one particular dimension (D, I, S, or C) **on a consistent basis.**

For example, if someone you know, seems to always be in a hurry, talks fast, might not naturally smile too often, and tends to speak her mind with little or no inhibitions (but without using stories or humor), sticking mostly to the bottom line, this person is most likely a "**Dominance (D) Style**" individual. You'll find the behavioral tendencies of this style described in detail in Chapter 4.

If someone around you talks fast, moves fast, loves to tell stories and is humorous; as well as smiles most of the time, this person is most likely an **"Influence (I) Style"** individual. You'll find the behavioral <u>tendencies</u> of this style described in detail in Chapter 5.

Another behavioral style that tends to smiles a lot, but in a more subtle way, is the **"Steadiness (S) Style"**; however, this person is more moderate paced both when talking and completing tasks or activities. The S Style is the best listener of all behavioral styles, is extremely supportive and friendly, and is more likely to abide by rules and traditions than either the D or the I style individuals. You'll find the behavioral <u>tendencies</u> of this style described in detail in Chapter 6.

Finally, you'll recognize the **"Conscientiousness(C) Style"** individual by their tendency to be more reserved and cautious most of the time, talk at a more moderate pace, think of life as "serious business," take the tasks they work on more seriously than any of the other styles, and are very particular about details, accuracy, and following rules. You'll find the behavioral <u>tendencies</u> of this style described in detail in Chapter 7.

‼ The beauty of the *Behavioral Style* concept is that it does not necessarily lock anyone rigidly in one style or another, but teaches us that we can flex our style, enabling most of us to adopt different behavioral styles as needed in different situations. For example, one might display a different behavioral style while at home talking to one's spouse or child, and a different behavioral style while at work. Even at work, one might adopt a different style when interacting with a pleasant coworker vs. when interacting with a strict manager or a coworker who is perceived as difficult; and might adopt a different style while providing service to a customer.

> The beauty of the *Behavioral Style* concept is that it does not necessarily lock anyone rigidly in one style or another, but teaches us that we can flex our style, enabling most of us to adopt different behavioral styles as needed in different situations.

‼ While we can all flex – or adapt - our behaviors as needed, based on different situational needs, <u>we all have a dominant *behavioral style*</u> that is observable on a daily basis. A person's **dominant *behavioral style*** is determined by one's tendency to display behaviors from one particular style (D, I, S, or C[1]) on a consistent basis.

---

[1] - The four styles are described in Chapters 4, 5, 6, and 7

Understanding Your Behavioral Style

As we talk about behavioral styles it is important to note (again) that nobody is purely one style or another. Even those who take a DISC profile[1] (or assessment) and find that they are purely one particular style will find themselves adopting regularly behaviors from the other three styles (and especially from the two adjacent ones). We all possess the ability to adopt behaviors from each style and most of us do adopt behaviors from

Once you learn about your behavioral style and become aware of your natural strengths and weaknesses, you can choose to reach more into the adjacent behavioral dimensions that will aid you in becoming more effective in any given situation.

different styles to fit the demands of the different situations we face.

For example, if someone is a high D – outspoken and determined – who tends to be driven, focused on goals and tasks, and spends little time nurturing relationships; when needed, this person will – or can, if he or she chooses to – take time to socialize and perhaps even be humorous (I style behavior), get organized and focus 100 percent on quality (C style behavior), or be kind and caring (S style behavior).

The same is true for the other three styles: each style has the ability to adopt behaviors from the other styles as required by different situations. Well.., with some limitations.

I'm sure you noticed that some behaviors come more naturally to you, while others take some real effort. For some of us socializing comes naturally, while for others it feels like a dreadful stumbling block; for some, attention to detail comes naturally and seemingly with ease, while for others it is a constant struggle. Some of us are great at listening to others' complaints, joyful stories, etc., while others have to force themselves to listen, and more often then not, they'll interrupt the speaker and/or find an excuse to leave.

Once you learn about your behavioral style and become aware of your natural strengths and weaknesses, you can choose to reach more into the adjacent behavioral styles to aid you in becoming more effective in any given situation.

---

[1] - To take the validated and reliable DiSC® Classic Profile, and view a brief description of it online, visit **www.egSebastian.com/disc_classic**

Yes, you will most likely find that you feel more comfortable adopting behaviors from one particular style – or styles – but with that awareness, you will be empowered to choose to adopt behaviors from the other styles, aiding you in becoming more effective in building your relationships and be more effective at accomplishing your goals.

Understanding Others' Behavioral Styles

Learning about the behavioral styles of others will allow you to instantly recognize the different styles in your environment and understand why each behaves as he or she does, giving you an edge on facilitating your communication with everyone around you.

Often you will recognize a specific behavioral style – D, I, S, or C - in the individuals around you; some people, however, will display behaviors from a combination of two, or even three, styles. In this case interpreting the person's behavioral style can be more challenging, but with little practice anyone can identify combinations of styles, such as DC, SC, ISC, SCD[1], etc.

A good place to start is to get a good understanding of each of the four behavioral styles. So let's get more familiar with our general behavioral tendencies by first exploring some common characteristics of the styles.

Remember!
No behavioral style is better or worse! Each and every style has its strengths and weaknesses. You can become the "best you" when you get a good understanding of your style, learn to capitalize on your strengths, and – if you choose to – work on some of your weak areas. You are already perfect as you are – you just have to use your gifts to your advantage.

---

[1] - - Visit **www.egSebastian.com/15** to learn more about the 15 Behavioral Styles Blends If you completed a DiSC® 2.0 or DiSC 2Plus profile, you can find a detailed description of the 15 Behavioral Style Blends on the last 6 pages of your profile

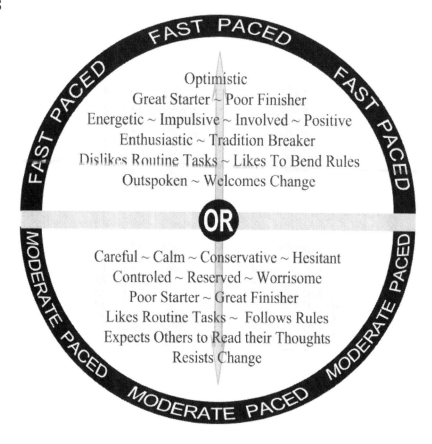

Figure 3.2 – Behavior tendencies based on a person's *Pace*

Common Characteristics of the Four Behavioral Styles

When it comes to human behavior, people can be categorized by a myriad of criteria: extrovert/introvert, outgoing/reserved, active/passive, accepting/questioning, impulsive/careful, etc., etc.

However, for the sake of simplicity, AND because that's all we need for our purposes, we'll consider only two such criteria that will help us recognize different behavioral styles. These two criteria also give us the two axes that will help us build the DISC model:

1. **Vertical Axis**: Is this person *Faster Paced* or more *Moderate Paced?* (Fig 3.2)

   AND

2. **Horizontal Axis**: Is this person *People Oriented* or more *Task Oriented?* (Fig. 3.3)

Simply by noticing a one's pace, one can safely expect a whole set of behaviors (Fig 3.2):

Fast Paced People tend to talk fast, move fast, and often come across as confident individuals; while also **tend** to consistently display the following behaviors:
- make quick decisions
- are often impulsive
- are positive and expect things to turn out right
- are great at starting projects; not always great at finishing projects
- are enthusiastic and more energetic (than moderate paced people)
- they are impulsive and get involved easier in whatever goes on around them (including conflict)
- often tradition breakers
- believe rules were made to be broken (or at least bent)
- love change

Moderate Paced People tend to talk at a slower pace, move slower, and often come across as reserved or even shy; while they also **tend** to consistently display the following behaviors:
- are hesitant and take their time to make decisions
- can be (a bit) worrisome (often about trivial matters)
- are poor starters of new projects
- great finisher (once they do start something, they make sure to bring it to completion)
- are more reserved, and at times might even come across as shy
- they have ability to focus on the project they work on, and are less interested in getting involved with other "distractions"
- calm and controlled
- conservative – respect traditions
- believe rules were made to be followed
- expects others to read their mind (they often do not express their wants, needs, or hurts, but rather expect those around them to somehow magically guess what's going on in their mind)
- they like stable environments and often resist change

The second criteria that will help you recognize a person's DISC style, is a person's tendency to be more *People Oriented* or *Task Oriented*. By simply noticing these tendencies, we can again safely expect some very specific behavioral tendencies. (See Fig. 3.3)

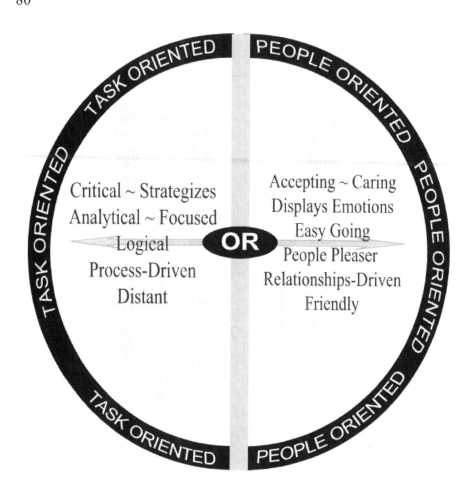

Figure 3.3 – Behavior tendencies based on a person's *People* vs. *Task Orientation*

Task-Oriented People

Task-oriented individuals (Fig. 3.3) enjoy working with tasks, concepts, numbers, etc. They also **tend** to <u>consistently</u> display the following behaviors:

- like to plan ahead, and derive satisfaction from developing and implementing processes
- have a natural tendency to be analytical

- will give 100% attention to the tasks they are working on, and they do not like to socialize while working on a task
- tend to approach things in a logical manner
- tend NOT to give much importance to – or display – "soft" emotions
- tend to be judgmental and critical of other's behaviors
- question the validity or accuracy of information they hear or receive
- due to the high focus on task-completion, they can come across as distant, cold, or unfriendly

People-Oriented People

People-oriented individuals (Fig. 3.3, pg 80) enjoy socializing and working with others. They also **tend** to <u>consistently</u> display the following behaviors:
- tend to be more accepting of people's behaviors
- tend to be more accepting of what they hear
- genuinely care about coworkers, friends, family members, and even total strangers
- derive great satisfaction from working with people
- are in touch with their emotions and they often express their emotions freely in conversations
- are very approachable, easygoing, and friendly
- have great sense of humor and are always ready to entertain or be entertained
- truly enjoy helping others and can come across as "people pleasers"
- due to high focus on developing and maintaining good relationships, task completion can become of secondary importance (which can make them look a bit sloppy at times)
- cry at sad movies

By joining these two axes: 1) *Pace*-based tendencies and 2) *Task* vs. *People* orientation tendencies, we get the DISC Behavioral Model (See Fig. 3.1 on 73). Chapters 4 through 7 will describe in detail each style.

Common Characteristics: A Humorous Look ☺

Funny and Practical "Facts":
Fast Pace vs. Moderate Paced individuals

	Fast Paced (D & I Styles)	Moderate Paced (S & C Styles)
When driving...	Always drive at the maximum speed "allowed" (around 10 mph above speed limit)	Drive at – or below – the maximum allowed speed
When driving up to a traffic light that just turned yellow...	Will accelerate, trying to make it before it turns red	Will stop, even if they are almost under the traffic light
When working...	High energy and enthusiastic, combined with little patience. Tend to task-hop.	Steady work-pace, with low enthusiasm. They will finish what they started.
When bringing decisions...	Act first - think later. They make decisions on impulse.	First think... think... think... then act. They make decisions once they have considered all angles.
When approaching tasks...	Just Do It! ... and learn as they go. They often apply "creativity" when completing tasks, often using their intuition, or best guess, to proceed. When building something and they have a few extra parts left, they are happy that the manufacturer provided spare parts.	Read the instructions and/or do thorough research before proceeding. They follow instructions to the letter. When building something and they have an extra part left, they'll spend hours trying to figure out where that part belongs.
When cooking...	Can never cook the same food twice – each time applies creativity to the recipe	Follows recipe each time to the letter (why reinvent the wheel?)
When eating...	Sometimes eats "on the move," while driving, or while working. Eats out a lot.	Sits down and eats "properly." Often plans ahead and prepares own food.
In social settings...	Smooth networkers	Can come across as shy and withdrawn

Funny and Practical "Facts":
Task Oriented vs. People Oriented

	Task Oriented C & D Styles	People Oriented S & I Styles
On the job...	Great at planning and executing tasks	Great at providing good customer service
	Great at completing tasks individually	Great at team-work
In communication...	Fact-based and bottom-line. Often lacks tact and finesse.	Considers others' feelings. Facts are of secondary importance.
	Question most things they hear	Accepting with most things they hear
	Blunt - will hurt others feelings (without being aware of it)	They genuinely care about others' feelings and try not to offend anyone
	Maintains a serious facial expression; seldom smiles	Tend to smile every time someone talks to them
Tend to bring decisions based on...	Logic and facts	Feelings and emotions
Expressing emotions...	Guarded and inexpressive	Open book. Expresses emotions freely (cries at sad movies)
They see the world ...	In black and white (they live guided by logic and facts)	In color (they live guided by emotions and feelings)
When in conflict...	Outspoken and direct (The D will be blunt; the C will be more diplomatic, or might not express their frustration at all, till it "over-boils")	Will try to avoid conflict with whatever means necessary. Might swallow insults and injustices in order to maintain peace
They enjoy...	Working on projects	Socializing

84

 Attention!

The **DISC Behavioral System** was not designed to label the individuals around us. Its sole purpose is to help us better understand our own behavior and the behaviors of those around us and use this understanding to improve our communication with everyone.

The behaviors listed under each style are purely strong tendencies. Often people learn to improve upon their weaknesses and adopt behaviors from neighboring behavioral dimensions to make them more effective at creating successful relationships; and become more effective at setting and accomplishing goals.

How to Recognize Different Behavioral Styles

The "magic" of the DISC Behavioral Model is that there is no magic to recognizing the DISC styles of those around you. As you saw it in the information covered in the previous sub-chapter, it is rather easy for anyone to recognize a few observable behaviors that would give away a person's behavioral style.

One of the most obvious and easily observable differences in one's behavioral style is the pace at which a person talks, moves, and brings decisions. Then, with a little conversation and observation of a person, we can identify whether this person is more *People Oriented* or *Task Oriented.*

Here's a recap of what to look for:

If someone is...

Fast Paced **and** *Task Oriented,* this person would be called a Dominance (D) style individual (See Fig. 3.5, next page)

Fast Paced **and** *People Oriented,* this person would be called an Influence (I) style individual

Moderate Paced **and** *People Oriented,* this person would be called a Steadiness (S) style individual

Moderate Paced **and** *Task Oriented,* this person would be called a Conscientiousness (C) style individual

---

At times all it takes is a few minutes of conversation with someone – or observing someone in their interaction with others - and we can get a clear idea of that person's behavioral style based on that person's pace and task vs. people orientation. At other times it can take longer to "read" a person's behavioral style.

As I mentioned earlier, nobody is purely D, I, S, or C style. We are all a combination of two or more of the styles at different intensities, and that's what makes those around us so diverse. And while we all are a blend of each of the four styles, most of us have a highly recognizable dominant style that is expressed most of the times. That is when we are in surroundings where we feel comfortable enough not to put on the mask of compliance – the mask that we wear to satisfy others' expectations of us.

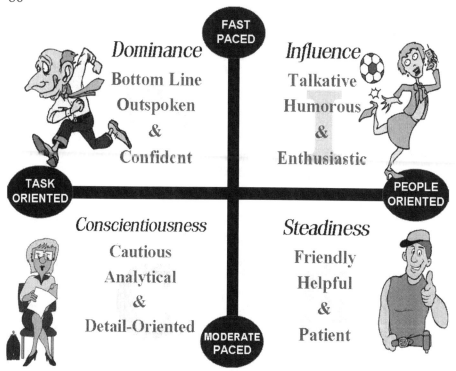

Figure 3.5 – Easily recognize the four styles based on *pace,* and *task vs. people* orientation

When "reading" people's behavioral styles, we'll usually notice a person's dominant style, which usually is all we need in order to communicate more effectively with those around us.

For example, if someone is fast paced, totally focused on what they do, seem not to welcome socializing (at that moment), and talk in brief and to-the-point sentences **(D Style)**, you'd know not to waist this person's time with stories and humor, but rather keep the conversation short, focused, and bottom line. (See more in Chapter 4, *The Dominance Style*)

On the other hand, if someone is fast paced and seems to love to socialize, freely share their stories, and are humorous **(I Style),** feel free to share your own stories and be humorous yourself; or simply listen with a smile and occasionally comment on what is being said. You'll soon learn that when talking to I style individuals, you don't have to talk much – they'll do most of the talking. But they do expect you to smile and nod enthusiastically as you listen to their stories and humor. (See more in Chapter 5, *The Influence Style*)

When you find that someone is more moderate paced, listens well, smiles, and comes across as kind and supportive (**S Style**), you'll find that this person will always be there for you to listen to your stories, humor, or problems; and will listen well and try to support you in any way he or she can. You'll also find that this person is hesitant to do anything outside of his or her routine and resists change, hence you'd not try to dump on them sudden changes, nor request them to do things that they don't feel comfortable with. (See more in Chapter 6, *The Steadiness Style*)

When you'll meet individuals who are moderate paced, and who clearly seem less interested in socializing and are more focused on task-oriented activities, (**C Style**), you'll want to keep your conversation focused, bottom line, and be prepared to listen to some in-depth information. You'll notice that this style devotes considerable time on becoming really good at what they do and put lots of thought into their actions; therefore, when they share, you should better be ready to listen well[1]. (See more in Chapter 7, *The Conscientiousness Style*)

It is important to note that most of us are somewhere in between the two extremes on both axis. Needless to say that it is the easiest to recognize the DISC style of people who "live" on the extremes of each axes; that is, the people who are either very fast-paced or very slow paced; AND are either very sociable – people oriented – or tend to spend their lives on task-related activities (crunch numbers, conduct research, build computers or other gadgets, plan, strategize, are process driven, etc.)

It is harder to read the people who display *Pace* and *Orientation*[2] tendencies that are close towards the middle of BOTH axes. As long as a person displays strong behavioral tendencies at least on one of the two axes, you'll be able to use what you learned in this book to

> It is important to remember that the purpose of reading a person's style is not to label that person – its sole purpose is to use that understanding to communicate more effectively with those around you.

---

[1] - Just like the S Style, C style individuals do not like sudden changes and like to follow set routines

[2] - *People* vs. *Task* orientation

communicate more effectively and maintain a successful relationship with this person.

You will notice that most people will be rather easy to read. Some people will "give away" their behavioral style in a few seconds in a conversation, or even before they start speaking:

D Style – you recognize them as they walk fast, move fast, and have a determined look – they often talk in brief sentences and can be quite blunt at times

I Style – are easily recognized as they move fast, have a big smile, expressive face and eyes, are talkative and humorous, and use expressive body language (when they see you, they might raise their hands high up, or motion as if ready to give you a hug, etc.)

S Style – can be recognized as they move "comfortably," seem constantly calm (even lethargic at times), might display a slight smile, and their face almost radiates the message "I'm kind and approachable"

C Style – can be recognized by their moderate pace, their intense focus as they get involved in a task, and might keep a serious facial expression even when someone approaches them to initiate a conversation with them

When initiating a conversation, the I and the S styles will naturally smile; while the pure, high D's and C's tend to keep a "poker" face or even a tensed face, almost like saying "Why are you bothering me?" Of course, depending on the environment, even the high D's and C's will (learn to) smile and be approachable. And since most of us are a combination of styles, most **D**s and **C**s are a combination with I or S styles, hence will be more sociable and smile more often.

It is important to remember that the purpose of reading a person's style is not to label that person – it's sole purpose is to use that understanding to communicate more effectively with that person. If, for example, you work in management position, that knowledge can be "translated" into communicating more effectively, being able to motivate your subordinates with more ease, or use this knowledge to help your subordinates become more productive. (See Chapters 4, 5, 6, and 7 for more on how to motivate each style)

Organizations of all sizes use assessments[1] to learn about their employees' DISC behavioral style. Often, these companies also provide DISC training to their employees and management teams to help them improve communication, team-effectiveness, reduce conflict, and improve productivity.

Now that we can easily recognize the D, I, S, and C styles, let's take a brief look at some of the general tendencies of each style.

General Tendencies of the Four DISC Styles

We all behave as we behave at any given moment for one of two reasons: 1) to gain pleasure or 2) to avoid pain. It's that simple.

The complexity of this "simple equation" comes in when we take in account that most of us perceive different things as "pleasure" or "pain". Some of us totally love to be in charge and associate pleasure and satisfaction with it, while

> While we all do what we do to gain pleasure or to avoid pain, we are still infinitely different due to our perception of what "pleasure" and "pain" mean to each of us individually.

others perceive it as a total painful and uncomfortable task and associate frustration and discomfort with it. Some of us love repetitive tasks – be that crunching numbers for hours everyday, working on an assembly line, providing telephone customer service for endless hours, etc. – while others will do their outmost best to avoid such tasks.

So, while we all do what we do to gain pleasure or to avoid pain, we are still infinitely different due to our perception of what is "pleasure" and what is "pain." And in spite of all our vast differences, we all have behaviors that are highly predictable, based on ones personality or behavioral style.

In chapters 4, 5, 6, and 7 we'll explore in depth each behavioral style, but before we jump into the thick of it, here is a quick overview of the four styles (Figure 3.6, on next page):

---

[1] - Visit **www.egSebastian.com/assessments** for more info

Fast Paced

AND

AND

Dominance

- Outspoken
- Wants to Control
- Results Oriented
- Process-Driven
- Decisive
- Leads by Example

Can come across as
- Cold
- Pushy
- Inconsiderate
- Aggressive

Influence

- Enthusiastic
- Talkative
- Easygoing
- Relationship-Driven
- Involved
- Humorous

Can come across as
- Impulsive
- Disorganized
- Tiring
- Fake

OR

Task Oriented

People Oriented

Conscientiousness

- Cautious
- Organized
- Analytical
- Quality-Driven
- Accurate
- Dependable

Can come across as
- Distant
- Perfectionist
- Nitpicky
- Antisocial

Steadiness

- Supportive
- Friendly
- Cooperative
- Stability-Driven
- Great Listener
- Calm

Can come across as
- Slow
- Passive
- Hesitant
- Easily Manipulated

AND

AND

Moderate Paced

Figure 3.6 – General Behavioral Tendencies of the Four Styles

By now you surely started recognizing the different styles in your environment. You probably noticed that most people around you are consistently investing some effort to work on their weaker areas; while others seem to totally give in to their natural tendencies.

While it is not always easy to put up with different styles' weaknesses, at least by now you've learned that those behaviors are not displayed to annoy you or anyone in particular, but it is rather due to each person's natural wiring. It is not personal – everyone is doing their best with what they have.

Important!
Do not use your newly found self-knowledge as an excuse!
As you read through the pages of the book and start getting a better understanding of your strengths and weaknesses, use what you learn to help you become more effective, both at communicating with others and at accomplishing goals. Do not use this knowledge to justify your ineffective behaviors by throwing your hands to the sky and say "Well, that's simply how I am!":

D styles – try to slow down (at least once in a while), show empathy, and take a conscientious effort to listen deeply to those around you

I styles – try to talk less (and do more), listen more, and continuously work on your planning and "staying organized" skills

S styles – practice being more assertive and take initiative

C styles – understand that not everything needs perfection; work on your people skills by trying to become more accepting and supportive with those around you

* Chapters 4 through 7 explores in detail each of the four styles and each chapter has a section that suggests specific ways on how each style can become more productive and more successful at creating and maintaining successful relationships

DISC Statistics

According to research[1] performed, by Inscape Publishing, Inc.[2], the approximate makeup of each behavioral style is as follows:

Pure Styles:

High D (Developer)	– 7%
High I (Promoter)	– 8%
High S (Specialist)	– 2%
High C (Objective Thinker)	– 7%

Combinations of Styles[3]:

DI (Inspirational)[4]	– 11%	SC (Perfectionist	– 16%
DI (Result-Oriented)	– 8%	SD (Achiever)	– 1%
DC (Creative)	– 18%	SI (Agent)	– 2%
ID (Persuader)	– 5%	SDC (Investigator)	– 1%
IS (Counselor)	– 5%	CIS (Practitioner)	– 5%
IC (Appraiser)	– 4%		

When we look at each style - regardless whether a style is purely D, I, S, or C, or in combination with other styles - it is interesting to notice that most styles are represented in our environment in almost equal numbers. (The totals do not add up to 100% because most of us are a

[1] - Source: "DiSC® Facilitator Report," by Inscape Publishing. The research has been performed on a sample population of more than 20,000 individuals. To see the demographic brake-down of the participants, you can request Inscape research reports by contacting support@egSebastian.com

[2] - Inscape is the world's leading provider of DiSC® assessments and other DiSC-based products (facilitator kits, action planners, etc). See **www.egSebastian.com** for a detailed list of Inscape DiSC solutions

[3] - The first letter stands for the primary style; for example: DI = scored highest in the Dominance style and scored 2nd highest in Influence style.

[4] - Visit **www.egSebastian.com/15** to learn more about the 15 Behavioral Styles Blends If you completed a DiSC 2.0 or DiSC 2Plus profile, you can find a detailed description of the 15 Behavioral Style Blends on the last 6 pages of your profile

combination of two or more styles and that's reflected in the overlapping data above.)

You Are in Charge of Your Behavior

The beauty of the DISC Behavioral System is that it promotes the ability to *choose* appropriate behaviors from the D, I, S, or C set of behaviors depending on what behaviors different situations require. Regardless of your behavioral style, you can choose to adapt to any particular situation by "borrowing" behaviors from any of the four styles.

And while most of us already do this instinctively, there are also some deeper underlying "forces" that play a role here. Before we choose to take the effort to adapt behaviors from any of the neighboring behavioral styles, the questions that arise in our subconscious are 1) do I have enough motivation to choose the "appropriate" set of behaviors in this situation (if I don't, I can get fired, I lose respect, get into a major unwanted conflict, etc), or 2) are the behaviors that seem appropriate in the moment in line with my natural behavioral style?

If the answer is yes to any of those questions, we'll do what seems right in the moment; but if the behaviors that are thought of as "appropriate" are not in line with our natural style, nor are there any strong incentives to motivate us to apply those behaviors, most of us, by default, go with our natural style.

I have met people who at work were very courteous with clients, displaying great patience and good listening skills (adopt behaviors that seem appropriate in the moment); yet in their home environment they tended to be jumpy, short-fused, and explosive, having almost daily arguments and conflict (allowed their natural style to take over completely – probably a sky high D, in this case).

Others are the exact opposite. I've met managers who at work are really decisive, demanding, and even loud and aggressive; yet at home they are really calm, humorous, patient, or straight out quiet and withdrawn; and allow the spouse – or significant other - to be in charge (at least with most mundane matters).

What is going on with these people? It is almost like they live double lives.

Well, in a way, they do live a double life, as most of us do once in a while when it comes to "borrowing" behaviors from different behavioral styles. Individuals with great people skills (or/and who studied DISC or other personality style system) will adopt whatever behavior is needed in order to accomplish maximum results in any given situation. We can be like a chameleon[1] when it comes to adopting behaviors from the four styles. At least, that's what most effective communicators tend to do.

Yes, some people take pride in treating everyone the same way, but that is rarely effective. We all have different needs and want to be treated in a certain way. Some of us expect (and at times demand) others to respect our privacy and don't like it when others pry in our personal life (C style); while others are an open book and welcome mostly any personal questions (I style). Some expect others to bundle things up and express any problem in a polite way and with a smile (S style); while others expect those around them to tell them straight in their face whatever problem might arise, without softening or bundling up the information (D style).

> ...when you decide to adopt behaviors from the other three dimensions when facing people of different styles, that's when you'll become most effective at creating and maintaining successful relationships with everyone around you.

Most of us adapt our behaviors depending on the different situations we find ourselves in, and for most of us it is not a conscious choice - we just do it out of respect for those around us. Yet for others it is a challenge to flex their adaptive "muscles" and tend to be stuck rigidly in their behavioral style.

If you find that you are one of those people who is uni-dimensional (that is, you are stuck in consistently displaying behaviors only from one of the behavioral styles), you need to understand that at any moment you have the whole array of the behaviors from the other three styles at your fingertips as well. And when you decide to adopt behaviors from the neighboring behavioral styles, when facing people of different styles, that's when you'll become most effective at creating and maintaining successful relationships with everyone around you.

Think of the sets of behaviors in the four styles as four bowls of fruits; for example, a bowl of cherries, strawberries, blueberries, and grapes. You might prefer one fruit over another, but any of the fruits in

---

[1] - Chameleons adapt to their environment by changing their color into the color of their surroundings

the four bowls are available to you at any time. And while you might prefer cherries over the other fruits, you might choose to eat the other fruits for their nutritional benefits.

Same applies to the four sets of behaviors in the four behavioral styles. You naturally prefer adopting behaviors from one or two sets of behaviors (D, I, S, or C), but for the sake of more effective communication – and often for the sake of peace or to create a sense of connectedness - you can at any time reach in any of the styles and pick the behaviors that fit best the situation.

Some of these behaviors might not come naturally to some of us, but we can always choose to use them in order to maximize our communication effectiveness with those around us. Remember, simply reach in the appropriate set of behaviors of any of the four styles – just as you'd reach to get a different fruit from a different bowl - and pick the appropriate behavior – or set of behaviors - that will bring best results in any particular situation.

> We expect others to treat us the way _we_ _want to be treated_, it's just fair to try to treat others _as **they** want to be treated_

Would this be considered as deceptive or untrue to one's true self? Definitely not! Shouldn't we be consistent and treat everyone the same way? No, not by far… Just think about it – think about the people around you. Do you want everyone to treat you as they treat most people; or would you rather have those around you respect your needs and treat you as YOU want to be treated?

Fact is, we all want to be treated based on our needs and expectations. And as we expect others to treat us the way WE WANT TO BE TREATED, it's just fair to try to treat others AS THEY WANT TO BE TREATED. To accomplish this, you would simply learn to "flex" – or adapt – your behaviors in order to communicate most effectively and to accomplish maximum results in the shortest time.

For example, regardless of one's style, we all find ourselves needing to take charge once in a while, be decisive, and say it as it is (D); we find ourselves in situations when we enjoy telling a humorous story and just have a great time with those around us (I); we at times find ourselves kindly and patiently listening to someone's complaint or story (S); and we all find ourselves being real sticklers for details when needed, such as at tax time, or while helping someone solve a problem.

Do we have to fake those behaviors? No. We simply adopt those behaviors because in those situations that's what is needed in order to accomplish the results we seek. Same applies to our everyday situations while dealing with coworkers, family members, bosses, or anyone in our environment. You can "borrow" at any time *appropriate behaviors* from any of the DISC styles to bring about the most desired results.

Important!

The DISC Behavioral System was **NOT** designed to label or to judge the individuals around us. It is simply a tool that can help better understand your own behavior and the behavioral tendencies and needs of the people you interact with on a daily basis.

This understanding of behavioral tendencies and the needs of each style can help improve your communication and relationships with everyone around you.

Power Tip #3

Avoid judging others based on their <u>perceived</u> behavioral style!

Be careful no to label or judge those around you based on your new awareness of the DISC behavioral styles!

Recognizing the behavioral style of those around you is important and CAN BE extremely helpful, but can be highly disabling when used to judge others. Use this knowledge to enhance your communication and relationships with those around you, NOT to judge others.

NOTES: _____

Chapter 4

The Dominance Style

> Famous High D Examples
> The Dominance(D) Style – Quick Overview
> How to Easily Recognize a D Style Individual
> Jim, the Super Achiever
> Communication Style
> Strengths and Weaknesses
> Challenge Areas
> Knowledge is Power! Take control of your weaknesses!
> Expectations of Others
> How to Deal with Conflict when Dealing with a D Style Individual
> Dominance Style - Born "Leaders"
> How to Motivate the D Style Individual
> What Demotivates the D Style Individual
> D's Most Popular Career Choices
> Power Tip #4: Keep Your D Styles Busy
> Dominance Style: Self-Coaching Worksheet

Famous High D Examples:

- Martin Luther King[1]
- Hilary Rodham Clinton
- Harrison Ford
- Denzel Washington (in *Déjà Vu, American Gangster, Inside Man…*)
- Robert De Niro (in *Analyze This* [DI], *Showtime, The Mission…*)
- Al Pacino (*The Recruit, The Insider, City Hall…*)
- Madonna (the singer)

---

[1] - DC combination

The Dominance (D) Style – Quick Overview

> **Dominance (D) –** *fast paced* **and** *task oriented*
> D's are determined and dynamic people who like to take charge, bring quick decisions, and want quick results

- ☑ Do you tend to move fast, talk fast, and bring quick decisions?
- ☑ Do you prefer planning and working on tasks, concepts, and ideas? (vs. spending most time interacting with others)
- ☑ Are you more interested in working on projects and performing hands-on activities that lead to accomplishing goals?
- ☑ Do you tend to be outspoken and blunt?
- ☑ Do you enjoy setting and accomplishing goals?
- ☑ Do you tend to be inpatient and demanding with those around you?
- ☑ Do you like challenges?
- ☑ Do you like to be in charge?

If you answered "yes" to most of these questions, then you most likely are a high D –Dominance - style[1] individual, or a combination of two or more styles with some high D traits.

Or perhaps you know someone in your environment who fits this description. If yes, it is most likely that this person is a D style individuals and displays most of the behaviors described in this chapter.

---

[1] To get an accurate idea of what is your behavioral style, complete the valid and reliable DiSC® 2.0, DiSC 2Plus, or DiSC PPSS profile, at **www.egsebastian.com/disc_classic**

Figure 4.1 – D style individuals charge towards their objectives, powerfully like a tank, while also pushing those around them to take action

D style individuals are most easily spotted by noticing who in your environment has the drive and *attitude* of a high-speed tank. **Ds** are success- and results-driven individuals who tend to move towards their goals forcefully, often disregarding others' feelings or interests (just like a tank). Most **Ds** also have a rather explosive temper, which luckily many learn to control and are constantly trying NOT to step on others' toes.

Individuals who are faster paced and are more interested in dealing with tasks and concepts, tend to adopt mostly behaviors from this set of behaviors (see pg. 101) and we call them Dominance (D) Style individuals. This chapter describes in detail the behavioral tendencies of Dominance (D) style individuals.

When a person tends to adopt mostly behaviors from the Dominance (D) style set of behaviors on a consistent basis, this person would be called a
D Style individual
(or Dominance Style Individual)

– Fast Paced/Task Oriented –

The Dominance(D) Behavioral Style

Dominance style individuals tend to consistently adopt <u>most</u> of the following behaviors:

General Tendencies
- ☑ Likes high-speed environments
- ☑ Likes to set and accomplish goals
- ☑ Likes to overcome challenges
- ☑ Comes across as confident (at times even arrogant)
- ☑ Takes initiative
- ☑ Likes to be in charge
- ☑ Natural leader (can become dictatorial)
- ☑ Tends to bring quick decisions
- ☑ Effective problem-solver
- ☑ Once they make a decision they go for it with utmost determination
- ☑ Dislikes repetitive activities

Communication Style
- ☑ Tends to talk and move at a faster pace
- ☑ In conversations focuses on facts **vs.** emotions
- ☑ Tends to be inpatient
- ☑ Can be blunt and outspoken
- ☑ Can become verbally aggressive when provoked or when trying to get an "important" point across
- ☑ Challenges the status quo
- ☑ Challenges authority

<u>D Style Motto:</u> "Just do it!"

D style individuals are probably best characterized by their fearless, no-excuses, "just do it" attitude. When facing a challenge or obstacle, D style individuals are the type of people who will go through it, above it, around it, or under it – they will do whatever it takes till they make it happen.

Approximate percentage of high D style individuals in the US:

Men - 31%

Women 24%

D style individuals strive on change; hence they will take any opportunity to improve things in their environment and will take charge to make those changes happen.

When at work, they do not like to be interrupted with personal stories, jokes, or other non-job related chit-chat. D style individuals can often come across as if they were on a mission. They can spend days, weeks, months, and years on pursuing personal and professional goals; at times to the detriment of their social ties.

Outside of the job, **D**s have no problem socializing as long as others are patient enough to listen to their exciting "stories" – which usually will gravitate around job-related and/or task related topics. They are not very good at listening to other people's stories, especially when the stories involve long descriptions of emotionally charged events. While they want to be emotionally connected to others, they often find themselves unwilling to invest time in nurturing their relationships.

When they capitalize on their strengths, high D style individuals often become great achievers; when they abuse their strengths, they become workaholics and can alienate others due to their "obsession" with their work, quick temper, and blunt communication style.

Due to their strong determination and total focus towards accomplishing their short- and long-term goals, **D** style individuals can often seem a bit distant, pushy, and inconsiderate. What we need to understand, though, is that they do not mean to upset anyone around them; they just simply are so focused on their tasks and are so goal-driven that everything else often becomes of secondary importance in their lives.

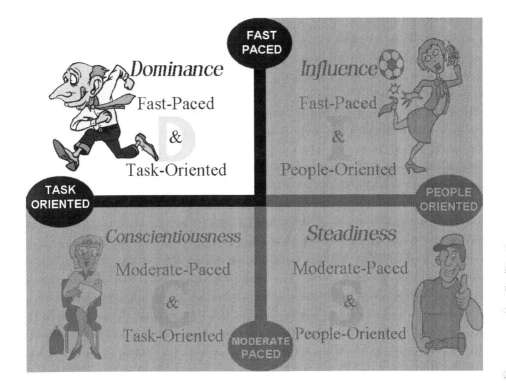

Figure 4.2 – The Dominance Style: Fast Paced & Task Oriented

How to Easily Recognize a D Style Individual

While most of us are a combination of two or more styles, most of us have a dominant style which is rather easy to spot.

It is rather easy to recognize the D Style individuals in your environment by noticing their fast pace and task orientation (Fig. 4.2).

They tend to move fast, talk fast, and bring decisions fast. They also love to set goals and they like to spend their days working on tasks that will take them closer to their goals. They are great at noticing flaws or problem areas and will take immediate action to fix – or have fixed - those deficiencies.

The D style individuals around us are the ones who make things happen in our environment, no matter what they set their mind to. They bring decisions quickly and move to action without hesitation. They are also the ones who move the rest of us to action – sometimes nicely and sometimes quite bluntly. **D**s are all about action – true leaders who stand out due to their courage, outspoken nature, and take-action-now attitude.

Jim, the Super Achiever

Jim[1]'s days start early every day of the week. He'll work out every morning at 5:30 at a community gym and he will arrive at his office sometimes between 6:45 and 7:00 am. He starts his day with planning.

Throughout the day he tries to follow his plan, though he often will modify the plan as he feels necessary. When he attends meetings, he speaks up, most of the time in a serious tone, and often challenges other people's views and ideas. He often raises his voice to make a point or to express strong criticism of ideas that he dislikes.

He maximizes every moment of the day and regularly sees new opportunities that he jumps on instantly. He is an avid investor, and whenever he sees an opportunity for a quick return, he invests with no hesitation. It is not rare that his investments net him tens of thousands of dollars within days. While he also, at times, loses considerable amounts of money on these deals, he is confident in his abilities, does not "invest" his emotions in his dealings, and he has a high tolerance for risk.

Jim is a construction engineer and owns a construction company. He used to do most of the designs himself, but now he hires other engineers to do his building designs and other complex planning. He enjoys spending his time getting new clients, while also often ventures out to unrelated money-making ventures.

While Jim has a beautiful wife and three children, most of the days he gets home at about 8:00 or 9:00 pm, and spends most of his week-ends hunting or on some other sports trips. He is a great provider for his family and once a year he spends 7 to 10 days traveling to a fancy vacation spot with his wife and children.

Jim is a great example of a **high** D style individual.

---

[1] - Not his real name.

Communication Style

- ☑ high D's are determined people who place more emphasis on accomplishing their goals and tend to spend less time on nurturing relationships
- ☑ are fast paced talkers
- ☑ they tend to speak with authority in their voice; hence they come across as confident; at times can come across as pushy and domineering
- ☑ are focused on the bottom line and accomplishing tasks or goals; they often take a conscious effort NOT to waist time on social niceties (though this is most of the time a natural tendency, rather than choice)
- ☑ they expect everyone around them to be focused and task oriented just like them, and when that's not happening they will often verbally – but often not very politely – encourage those around them to move to action
- ☑ they do not like to spend time on listening to stories, jokes, or unfocused chatter; nor do they like to engage in emotionally charged conversations
- ☑ they tend to be more interested in task oriented conversations, and definitely more interested in taking action than talking about taking action

Strengths and Weaknesses

Here are some of the D style strengths:

- ☑ quick decision maker
- ☑ believes in his or her abilities
- ☑ brave and fearless
- ☑ they have high tolerance to risk
- ☑ will speak up on issues that are important to them
- ☑ loves to plan and implement those plans immediately
- ☑ a born leader - likes to take charge and make things happen
- ☑ goal-oriented - they know what

It is important to note that each style's "strengths" are truly strengths when used in moderation. As uncle Ben said in the movie *Spiderman* "With great powers come great responsibilities" – and the same applies to each style's strengths...

they want and they go for it

- ☑ once they set their mind to something, usually they'll go for it 100% till they make it happen
- ☑ adventurous - manifested through regular traveling and hiking trips, participating in combat (or otherwise aggressive) sports, or getting involved in other high energy and entertaining activities
- ☑ outspoken – we always know how we stand with our **D**s
- ☑ is able to work in fast-pace and high-stress environments, where he usually gets great satisfaction out of staying on top of things
- ☑ loves to work individually
- ☑ works at a fast pace, is usually focused, and very productive
- ☑ notices areas needing improvement and instantly comes up with innovative ideas; wants to take action immediately on those ideas
- ☑ is competitive and achievement-driven
- ☑ great problem solver

It is important to note that each style's "strengths" are truly strengths when used in moderation. As uncle Ben said in the movie *Spiderman* "With great powers come great responsibilities" – and the same applies to each style's strengths. Our strengths are perceived as such only when we keep them under control (or when used responsibly, to use uncle Ben's term). Out of control, regardless of what style one might be, our strengths become weaknesses.

Our weaknesses are often nothing else but our strengths pushed to extremes. Yes, most often it is that simple; however, at times the very behaviors that we think of *strengths* can be perceived by others as weaknesses, no matter to what degree we use them.

Most of the conflict, misunderstandings, or other types of challenges that we get into, are most often the result of allowing our strengths to get out of control. Most of us know our weaknesses and we try to stay away from behaviors that make them surface. More often than not, however, it is our strengths – pushed to extremes - that get us in trouble.

> Your *weaknesses* are often the result of allowing your *strengths* to get out of control.

Here's a list of some of the D style individuals' strengths that can turn into weaknesses when allowed to get out of control:

Strengths UNDER Control	Strengths OUT OF Control
Adventurous	*Reckless / Impulsive*
Brave	
Ambitious	*Back-stabbing / Pushy / Dissatisfied / Fanatical / Workaholic*
Assertive	*Pushy / Demanding / Bossy / Dictatorial*
Leader	
Competitive	*Cruel / Merciless / / Hard-headed*
Confident	*Arrogant / Disrespectful*
Controlled	*Cold / Emotionless*
Determined	*Aggressive / Stubborn*
Independent	*Disregards others' opinions, input, etc.*
Goal Oriented	*Workaholic / Obsessive*
Productive	
High Achiever	
Honest	*Blunt / Sarcastic / Tactless / Offensive / Easily Angered / Argumentative / Defiant*
Outspoken	
Direct	
Innovative	*Challenges the status-quo / challenges authority*
Observant	*Fault-Finding*
Persistent	*Stubborn / Impatient*
Tough	*Inconsiderate / Emotionless / Intolerant*

Table 4.1 – Dominance Style: Strengths become weaknesses when pushed to extremes

Challenge Areas

- Dominance style individuals are highly driven and want to be high-achievers, but often neglect the human element and end up overlooking the importance of creating and maintaining successful social ties (both at work and at home)
- Love to take action but get easily bored with tasks that take too long to complete or require too much detail work
- Love others to listen to them, but are unwilling to listen to others
- At work they want to be respected; at home they want to be loved - but are **unwilling** to
  - listen carefully,
  - show emotions or empathy for others emotions,
  - accept others' strengths and weaknesses (are openly critical of others),
  - and often allow themselves to overpower others in a dictatorial manner
- They believe they are always right. They want others' input, but often, without even meaning, they discourage others from sharing ideas by verbally overpowering them and dismissing or harshly criticizing their ideas.
- They have a difficult time working for non-assertive managers
- Have difficulty accepting authority, as well as following rules and regulations; they like to do things their way. They like to work independently and be in control of their actions.
- They tend to be quick at noticing and pointing out faults, mistakes, irregularities, etc., which often creates conflict or tension with those around them
- Their trust in others' abilities is rather low; they want to do everything themselves and often have difficulty delegating
- They assume that due to their hard work, everyone loves them and accepts them as they are. The truth is that everyday people lose jobs and/or end up divorcing or breaking up due to lack of communicating with tact and finesse.
- They have difficulty working side-by-side with moderate paced individuals who are highly in touch with their emotions (S and SI style individuals). They get stressed by the other person's slow pace, hesitance, and regular emotion oriented communication.
- **D**s are often impatient, have a short fuse, and tend to lose their temper really easily. This can create a barrier to successfully creating and maintaining relationships with certain people around them (especially with S styles, but any other style as well)

Knowledge is Power! Take control of your weaknesses!

Nobody is perfect. Of course you heard that at least three million times this year alone; and while it does sound cliché, it is 100% true. Nobody is perfect – not even you. Sorry if that disappoints you.

And I do realize that if you are a D style, you might have thought that you were the alpha and omega, but I'm pretty sure that even you know that you have areas that can take some improvement work. Relax, we all do. We all have our strengths and weaknesses. And the good news is that most of our weaknesses are simply the result of abusing our strengths. Often we can simply take a conscious effort to tone down our strengths in order to become more effective at communicating with those around us.

Understand that most of your strengths – fast paced, bottom line, driven, etc. - are your best allies in accomplishing your goals, but at the same time , they are the very traits that can make you less effective in maintaining successful relationships.

Here are some areas where D's can take a conscious effort to bring about some improvement:

- Control your urge to tell those around you what to do or what not to do (except if you are in a leadership position – but even then give your subordinates a chance to think for themselves whenever possible)
- Try to realize that your way is not the only way; allow those around you to feel more *free* around you (not threatened, not judged, controlled by you, or nagged by you)
- Once in a while make a conscious effort to slow down and listen to those around you – that is really listen[1] (put your judgments aside, control your urge to give advice or dismiss what you hear, remain calm and smile, etc.)
- Think about possible consequences before you jump into things (or before you get into an argument with someone)
- When working (or socializing) as part of a group, try to step back once in a while and let others take charge
- When explaining a project or process, try to slow down and don't just blurt out the bottom line. Make sure to present it in enough

[1] - See pg. 45, *Effective Communication Starts with Effective Listening,* for more on listening skills

detail so everyone will understand how you got to your final conclusion.

- Consider other people's feelings! Understand that others might be more in touch with their emotional world and expect some empathy and tact from you

- Try not to use others' every little slip up as a reason to pick a fight. Pick your fights wisely; or even better, practice self-control and stop verbally overpowering those around you. Your actions and attitude already show those around you that you are not someone to mess with; use your verbal "powers" sparingly.

- When bringing decisions or changing a course of action, take a conscious effort to communicate it clearly with those who will be affected by your new course of action

- In your pursuit for accomplishment and on-the-job advancement, try not to step on others' toes – this can be really counterproductive in the long run

- Accept the fact that we are all different and possess different strengths. Raise your acceptance levels of those around you by learning to appreciate the strengths of each style (and, if you are in management, capitalize upon those strengths).

- Try to criticize less and support more. Some people around you need your support, and they need you do it with patience and some warmth. If you are in management position, understand that some employees (especially S style) might be intimidated by your dynamic and straightforward personality. They need you to slow down a bit and talk to them in their "language" (S style "language": slow down, smile if possible, listen carefully, and provide detailed instruction on what needs to be done and HOW you expect it done). If you are a parent, this is probably a most important area for you to be aware off, especially if your kids are of any of the other three styles. Read the description of the other styles and understand that each style approaches communication, task-management, and life in general differently – approaches that we do not control. Learn to accept your children's behavioral style and learn to speak the language of their style (have fun with the I, listen carefully and be nice to the S style child, and take time to build things and discuss things with your C style child).

- Praise and reward those around you when catching them doing a good job - especially if you are in a management position or a parent). Most people like to be praised for what they do right, and they'll do more of it when they feel appreciated.
- Understand that just because you think you are right, it does not automatically mean you are right. Keep an open mind and learn to listen better to what the other party has to say. And remember, not everything is *black* or *white.*
- Try to go for "win-win" when dealing with others – be that workplace conflict, a business deal, or an argument with a family member. In the long run it will serve you much better than the default "win-lose" behavior
- Learn some small-talk skills[1]; it will serve you greatly in the long run.
- If you have a *temper* problem (as most **Ds** do), learn some anger management techniques (often regular meditation and positive affirmations can take care of the problem). This is important for multiple reasons: for example, if you have regular outburst on the job, you'll be viewed as unstable and people will start avoiding you; and if you are a parent, you should make it a top priority to learn to control your temper for the sake of everyone involved.
- Commit to spend time regularly – at least weekly – with an S style person, and practice speaking their "language": slow down, listen to them, and smile as you listen or when you talk; sit down and lean back, relax. Learning S style behaviors is the key for you to improve your personal relationships. Capitalize on your S style acquaintances – learn from them!
- Relax! Spend time nurturing your relationships; and your mental and physical health.
- Dare to smile more often.
- Capitalize on your strengths and you'll be a high achiever; allow your strengths to get out of control, and you'll become antisocial and a workaholic.

---

[1] - Most D style individuals are great networkers and great at small talk, but small talk does not always come naturally to them – it is something that some Ds have to still realize why it is necessary and include it in their behavior repertoire. (Some D style individuals view small talk as non-sense, waste-of-time-chit-chat)

Expectations of Others

Here's what D's expect from everyone around them:

- *Be brief and to the point – don't waist my time!*
- *If you have something to say* (as in, something negative or possibly conflict-triggering), *say it to my face, and don't dance around it. Just tell me as it is*
- *Listen to what I'm saying, and listen well ('cause I won't say it twice)*
- *Don't waist my time with chit-chat, jokes, stories, or "worthless" small talk- get to the point!*
- *You got a job to do, so just do it; do fast, and do it well*
- *Take initiative – be a self-starter!*
- *Be competent – know what you're doing – I don't have the patience to teach you.*
- *Be competent – know what you're talking about – I don't have the patience to listen to gibberish.*

When their expectations are not met, **D**s can become irritable, impatient, critical, and bossy with those around them. Just like every other style, they believe that everyone else should be just like them (fast paced, bottom-line, self-starters, driven, etc). Understanding the diverse nature of different behavioral styles will improve the **D**s acceptance levels of others, understanding that people around them are not weird, but simply differently wired.

How to Deal with Conflict when Dealing with a D Style Individual

- Run! You can't win. This is a behavioral style that can really *blow the lid off* and will fight like a tiger. Better wait till they calm down.
- An alternative to the above point is to stand your ground, but let them vent first – they will get more upset if you interrupt them – and then use logic and data to respond to their outburst; unless while listening you came to the realization that they are right, in which case feel free to agree with them. (They usually are very practical, though not always very thorough in planning their course of action; they often make things up as they go. They believe in "shoot" then 'aim" philosophy.)

- Best is to wait till they calm down; chances are that they will approach you to apologize and resolve the conflict in a civilized manner.
- Once they are calm you can share your side and ask them to try to view both sides in an objective manner (which they are incapable to do while in anger-mode).
- If you are a manager, supervisor, or in other leadership role: if you notice anger or disobedience, 1) let the person vent first AND/**OR** 2) stop him firmly and ask him to come back after he calms down.
- Do not try to appeal to their emotions! Questions such as "How would it make YOU feel, if I treated you this way" have no meaning to them.
- Do not try to persuade them through examples (stories) – they have no patience to listen to them, and while you talk, they'll either think of what they'll say, or most likely they'll interrupt you.
- The only way to persuade them (when they are calm) is through facts, data, numbers, and logic.

Remember!

In conflict, the truth is rarely "black" or "white" – more often then not both of you might be right; you just have to be willing to take time to understand each other's point of view and...

1. agree to disagree agreeably, or
2. come to the realization that the issue at hand can be viewed in multiple ways and you are both right, or
3. come up with a happy medium (compromise), or
4. synergize[1]: come up with a better *solution* than any of you originally had – a solution that will satisfy both of you

---

[1] - Steven Covey, Seven Habits of Highly Effective People. Simon and Schuster. New York, 1989 (pg 221)

Dominance Style - Born Leaders

High D style individuals are the ones who are called by many "born leaders." And while you will often hear that there's no such thing as a "born leader," High D style individuals are every bit of a leader – perhaps not always in the way as we think of the term "leader" and "leadership" these days, but they are definitely people who take charge without hesitation and lead those around them. Which, yes, sometimes it can translate into driving everyone crazy around them due to their high pace, lack of patience, desire to be in charge, and tendency to jump into things without weighing much the pros and cons.

Usually **D**s are more interested in forging ahead with their plans than worrying about how their actions and bottom-line-communication might affect those around them.

High D's are often very charismatic individuals due to their confidence and purpose-driven lifestyles. Unfortunately their "purpose-driven lifestyle" is not always positive (they could come across as pushy workaholics), which just shows that they are also just regular "mortals" like any one of us, except for them it comes a bit more naturally to take charge and lead others.

In a group environment high D's often end up becoming group leader, president, etc. and they will do an excellent job at getting things done.

Of course, as I stated in earlier chapters, anyone can reach into the D set of behaviors and choose to take control and lead. We all have met I, S, and C behavioral style individuals who are great managers, political leaders, or are filling some other type of leadership roles. Anyone can choose to take charge and lead – it is a question of will and motivation. It might not come naturally at first, but it's being done everyday by people of all personality/behavioral styles and there's no magic to it. Probably Nike would give you the best advice on this: Just do it!

Perhaps one major difference among the four styles when it comes to leadership (managing others) is that D style individuals not only can do a great job as managers, but they also enjoy it tremendously. The other three styles can also do a great job (while approaching it totally differently), but often they do not derive the same satisfaction as the D style individuals do.

How to Motivate the D Style Individual

Regardless whether we are talking about an employee, child, a spouse, or significant other, there are a few simple ways to motivate these highly driven individuals. While many of the suggestions below apply to motivating employees, there are also some that can be equally applied in other types of relationships.

- Let them feel in complete charge of projects - "I want you to be in charge," or similar statements are music to a **D**'s ears. They love to take initiative and not have to wait for others' approval.
- Give them bottom-line instructions, without over explaining – they like to feel that they came up with the main solution(s)
- Give them challenging tasks. **D**s get a great deal of satisfaction from overcoming challenging situations and from completing tasks that most find unattainable or stressful.
- Set tangible rewards for accomplishing goals, such as financial rewards, advancement opportunities, or increased authority.
- When working in teams, give the D style individual the authority to be in charge. Make them *team-leader, project leader,* or other title that would let team members know who is in charge. (The title is mostly necessary for team members – the D style employee will press forward and push others regardless whether they have a title or not. Having a title simply helps others know who is in charge of the project, hence be more accepting of the D's leadership; as well as let's the D style individual know that their efforts are appreciated.)

Remember!
Motivating others can be "tricky." You can ONLY motivate people to do things they are interested in. Trying to motivate different styles to complete tasks that are totally against their behavioral tendencies can be futile and ineffective. Take the effort to recognize the behavioral style of the person who you are working with and motivate them by allowing them to capitalize on their natural strengths[1].

---

[1] - Have your employee(s) take a DiSC® PPSS (or DiSC 2.0) to ensure that you get an accurate reading of the person's behavioral style. The DiSC profile will also suggest ways to motivate the person most effectively – for more details and to see a sample profile, visit **www.egSebastian.com/assessments**

What Demotivates D Style Individuals

- Working around overly verbose and unfocused individuals
- A slow environment that's void of opportunities for overcoming challenges and has no rewards for the **D**'s competitive and fast-paced nature
- Needing to report on every move they make
- Monotonous work
- A micro-managing manager or supervisor

D Style Most Popular Career Choices[1]

Professional Athlete	Bill Collector**	Financial Managers
Ambulance Driver	Corrections Officer	Construction Worker
Correspondent* or **	Courier	Court Reporters
Entrepreneur	Executive	Firefighter
Judge**	Farmer and Rancher	Agricultural Manager
First Line Supervisor	General Manager	HR Manager**
Financial Services Sales Agent **	Industrial Production Manager	Instructional Coordinator***
Construction Equipment Operator	Landscape Architect**	Painters (construction)
Emergency Medical Technician (EMS)	Medical Services Manager***	Police and Detective Supervisor
Interviewer** or ***	Journalist	Photojournalist
Paramedic	Personnel Recruiter*	Racecar Driver
Consultant**	Movie Director	Program Manager
Stucco Mason**	Producer	Stuntman
Project Manager	Purchasing Agent*	Sales Manager
Insurance (and other) Sales Agent* or **	Training and Development Manager*	Emergency Management Specialist (EMS)
Construction Manager	Customer Service Supervisor/Manager	Youth Program Director*
Architectural Engineer	Real Estate Developer	Ship and Boat Captain
Lawyer**	FBI/CIA Agent	Navy Seal
Drill Instructor	Police Officer	State Highway Patrol
Politician	Sports Coach	Public Speaker*
Deputy Sheriff	Probation Officer	Marketing Manager
Military[2] Serviceman	Military Officer	Pilot**
Carpenter	Real Estate Agent*	Actor
Foreman	Restaurant Manager	Reporter
Rap Artist	Rock Star*	Plasterer**

Table 4.2 – D Style Most Popular Career Choices

[1] - view a description of most of the above careers at **www.egSebastian.com/career**
[2] - US Army, Marine Corps, Navy, Air Force, Coast Guard…

* - often in DI combination
** - often in DC combination
*** - often in DCI combination

These are only a few of the careers most D's tend to enjoy, due to the fast-paced environments they provide, combined with plenty of opportunities to face and solve challenges.

If your behavioral style blend contains two (or three) styles at about the same intensity[1] levels, remember to check the most popular career choices for your secondary style as well. If, for example, you are a DC style individual, you'll probably enjoy several of the careers listed in the *C's Most Popular Career Choices* at the end of Chapter 7.

Power Tip #4

Keep your D styles busy!

Managers, Spouses, Teachers, & Parents: you better give your high D something to solve or "conquer," or else they'll end up blowing up in unexpected directions. Sky high **D**s are like a loaded gun that's ready to be fired, and if you don't aim them to the right target, they'll blow up in the wrong direction. S and C style managers, spouses and parents often expect their D style employee/spouse/child to conform to rules and "be nice." What you have to realize, though, is that the inner "engine" of the D is pushing them to take serious action, and if there's no action, they'll create it.

Get the **D**s in your life early on as your allies. Put them in charge of things. Keep them busy with challenging tasks and they'll be your most valuable allies in your life – people that you can depend on to make things happen.

---

[1] To get an accurate idea of what is your behavioral style, complete the valid and reliable DiSC® 2.0, DiSC 2Plus, or DiSC PPSS profile, at **www.egsebastian.com/disc_classic**

Dominance Style: *Improve Your Relationships and Effectiveness*
Self-Coaching Worksheet
(Print out a blank self-coaching sheet at **www.egSebastian.com/selfcoach**)

1. What are my strengths that I'm most proud of?

_____

_____

_____

2. What are some of my strengths that make me most effective in my
   environment?

_____

_____

_____

3. What are some of my strengths that are (perhaps) perceived as
weaknesses in my environment?

_____

_____

_____

4. What are some of my weaknesses that make me less effective in my
environment?

_____

_____

_____

5. Based on what I read in this chapter (and on what I already knew),
what can I do to become more effective at creating and maintaining
successful relationships in my workplace and/or at home? (Pages 109 -
111)

_____

_____

_____

6. Based on what I read in this chapter (and on what I already knew), what can I do to become more effective at setting and accomplishing personal and professional goals? (Pages 109 - 111)

_____

_____

_____

_____

_____

_____

_____

7. Is it an option to speak to my supervisor (or coworkers) and ask to be assigned tasks that are more in line with my strengths? If yes, how would I approach him/her/them about it?

_____

_____

_____

_____

_____

8. What else can I do to become more effective in all areas of my life? (Based on what you read – e.g., talk to spouse or significant other about your style and your style's needs, behavioral tendencies; how can you improve your relationship with loved ones, etc.)

_____

_____

_____

_____

_____

_____

_____

Remember!

Each of the four sets of behaviors are available to you!

Just like when having access to four bowls of fruits, you might prefer one fruit over the other, but it is up to you to reach in one or the other bowl and consume any of the four fruits.

The same applies to the four styles. They are at your fingertips at all times and it is up to you to reach in any of the four sets of behavior (D, I, S, or C) to make you more effective in any social situation. It might not always feel very comfortable or natural[1], but it is the most effective way to creating and maintaining successful relationships.

---

[1] - **D**'s have difficulty slowing down and listening well; I styles often have difficulty being bottom-line in delivering information; S styles often find it hard to be assertive and direct; and **C**s at times find it difficult to loosen up and socialize freely– when we become aware of these blind spots, we can take conscious effort to address them.

Chapter 5

The Influence Style

> Famous High I Examples
> The Influence (I) Style – Quick Overview
> How to Easily Recognize an I Style Individual
> Popular Cindy
> Communication Style
> Strengths and Weaknesses
> Challenge Areas
> Knowledge is Power! Take control of your weaknesses!
> Expectations of Others
> How to Deal with Conflict when Dealing with an I Style Individual
> Influence Style - The Source of Joy and Inspiration
> How to Motivate the I Style Individual
> What Demotivates the I Style Individual
> I's Most Popular Career Choices
> Power Tip #5: Hold I Styles Accountable to their Commitments!
> Influence Style: Self-Coaching Worksheet

Famous High I Examples:

- Whoopi Goldberg
- Robin Williams
- Edie Murphy
- Ellen DeGeneres
- Jim Carrey
- Jay Leno

The Influence (I) Style – Quick Overview

Influence (I) – *fast paced* **and** *people oriented*
I's are high-energy and enthusiastic people who like to influence others with their wit, humor, and persuasive skills

---

☑ Do you tend to move fast, talk fast, and are friendly with most people around you (even with total strangers)?

☑ Are you more people oriented? (vs. task oriented)

☑ Do you prefer spending most of your time interacting with others? (vs. working on tasks, concepts, dealing with numbers, researching, and planning)

☑ Do you consider yourself humorous, like to tell stories, jokes, or otherwise entertain others?

☑ Do you tend to get excited easily about new ideas and opportunities?

☑ Do you often end up being the center of attention (and usually enjoy it)?

☑ Do you often try to influence others through appealing to logic and emotions?

☑ Do you tend to be enthusiastic, upbeat, and sociable most of the time?

If you answered "yes" to most of these questions, then you most likely are a high I – Influence - style[1] individual. Or perhaps you know someone in your environment who fits this description. If yes, it is most likely that this person is an I style individual and displays most of the behaviors described in this chapter.

---

[1] To get an accurate idea of what is your behavioral style, complete the valid and reliable DiSC® 2.0, DiSC 2Plus, or DiSC PPSS profile, at **www.egsebastian.com/disc_classic**

Figure 5.1 – I style individuals are high-energy people who have an endless supply of enthusiasm and wit

I style individuals are most easily spotted by noticing who in your environment acts mostly like an entertainer or almost like a motivational speaker. I style individuals are (usually) charming and upbeat individuals who tend to take any chance to share their stories – often humorous ones – and jokes. They love to entertain those around them or to influence them towards acceptance of an idea or to encourage others to take action. To get a laugh, I style individuals don't mind making a fool out of themselves or use self-deprecating humor.

They are a powerhouse of passion, and their enthusiasm and wit is inexhaustible.

Most I style individuals have some challenges with staying organized and focus on complex tasks. Of course, most learn to control their natural unproductive behaviors and are constantly learning skills that help them become more organized and productive.

They are the ones who brighten up any environment (workplace, home, or other settings) with their enthusiasm, humor, positive attitude, and love for people. They are upbeat most of the time and are great at helping others see things in more positive ways. One of their main strength is the ability to influence others through their excellent verbal and people skills.

> **Approximate percentage of high I style individuals in the US:**
>
> Men - 23%
>
> Women 27%

I styles are all about relationships; they love to see everyone happy around them and will do whatever it takes to make that happen.

Individuals who are faster paced and are more interested in socializing and influencing others through their good verbal skills, tend to adopt mostly behaviors from this set of behaviors (pg.128) and we call them Influence (I) Style individuals.

This chapter covers in detail the behavioral tendencies of I style individuals.

Remember!
No behavioral style is better or worse! Each and every style has its strengths and weaknesses. You can become the "best you" when you get a good understanding of your style, learn to capitalize on your strengths, and – if you choose to – work on some of your weak areas. You are already perfect as you are – you just have to use your gifts to your advantage.

I style individuals tend to be masters of social skills and love to use those skills to accomplish their goals. They like to feel part of a group and like to be the center of attention; and they often end up being the center of attention regardless whether this was their purpose or not. They love to accomplish goals (mostly short-term goals) and get great satisfaction from being praised publicly for their accomplishments.

I style individuals are master communicators and persuaders. They are great at appealing to people's emotions and logic, and are the only style that is (usually) able to persuade others about whatever they set their mind to.

Because **Is** are so people oriented, they will do everything possible to avoid conflict. Unfortunately, due to their tendency to talk before they think, combined with their impulsiveness, they regularly end up hurting others' feelings or offending others. Usually, however, they are really quick to rectify their blunder with a quick joke or some witty explanation.

Whether on the job or at home, **Is** are friendly people who enjoy entertaining those around them, as well as they like to be involved in the lives of those around them and help them in whatever way they can (especially with advice).

I style individuals have a true love for people. They love to attend functions and parties and strike up new friendships with total strangers in a matter of minutes. They are the type of people who'll start talking to strangers in an elevator, while standing in line, while waiting for a green light to cross a street, or any other instance where there's a moment of silence around others.

They are very much in touch with their emotional world and have a high need to give and receive affection. Due to their regard for others feelings, **Is** are often not as assertive as they'd like to be.

While they want to be connected to others and want to feel needed, they at times alienate others by being too verbose, gossipy, over-promising and disorganized.

When they capitalize on their strengths, **Is** are wonderful and entertaining people - often the life of any party. When, however, they push their strengths to extremes, they become gossipy, annoying (too much talk and silly jokes), and unreliable (they want to help too many people – or try to accomplish too many things at a time - hence they have no time to fulfill all their commitments).

> **When a person tends to adopt mostly behaviors from the Influence (I) style set of behaviors on a consistent basis, this person would be called an**
> **I Style individual**
> (or Influence Style Individual)

– Fast Paced/People Oriented –
The Influence (I) Behavioral Style

Influence style individuals tend to consistently adopt **most** of the following behaviors:

General Tendencies:
- ☑ Tends to talk and move at a faster pace
- ☑ Dislikes repetitive activities
- ☑ Loves attention
- ☑ Loves to help others
- ☑ Loves to work in small teams
- ☑ Loves to be praised publicly for accomplishments
- ☑ Is positive
- ☑ Comes up with quick solutions to problems
- ☑ Tends to be disorganized and is often unrealistic
- ☑ Is great at starting projects; poor at finishing them
- ☑ Tends to hop from task to task
- ☑ Displays more confidence than what he can back up

Communication Style:
- ☑ Enthusiastic and easygoing
- ☑ Friendly and talkative
- ☑ Loves to interact with everyone around them (including strangers)
- ☑ Loves to entertain others – often becomes the center of attention
- ☑ Influences others by appealing to emotions and logic
- ☑ Is a poor listener; often interrupts others in mid-sentence
- ☑ Agreeable - has difficulty saying "No"
- ☑ Loves to help others – often is over-promising
- ☑ Tends to see humor in mostly everything
- ☑ At times gossipy
- ☑ Tends to exaggerate for the sake of humor or self-promotion
- ☑ Tends to smile most of the day

I style motto:
- ☑ "Let's have some fun!"

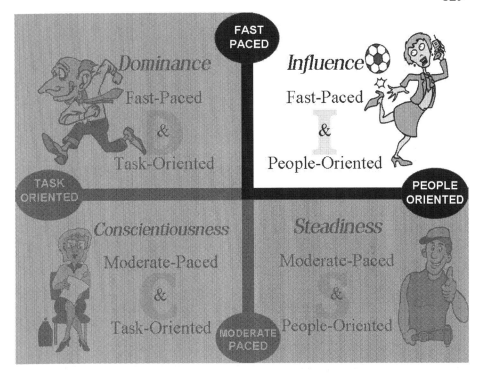

Figure 5.2 – The Influence Style: Fast Paced & People Oriented

How to Easily Recognize an I Style Individual

While most of us are a combination of two or more styles, most of us have a dominant style which is rather easy to spot.

Out of the four styles, the I style individuals are probably the easiest to recognize. Whether in a group setting or one-on-one, I style individuals can be spotted from far, due to their loud laughter, enthusiastic story telling, animated body language, and a constant sunny disposition.

I style individuals tend to move fast, talk fast, and love to socialize (Fig. 5.2). They love to spend their days in environments where they can use their good verbal skills. They are natural entertainers; they see humor in everything.

When you step into their office, or home, you'll see pictures of them with the company president, the governor, or some other highly regarded person or personality, and/or a ton of certificates of accomplishments. I's love to shine and they love to be viewed as someone competent and influential.

Popular Cindy

Everyone knows Cindy[1]!
And… everyone loves Cindy. Ok, maybe not everyone, but most people do. She is the type of person you either love or can't stand – nothing in between. She's a social butterfly: energetic, enthusiastic, entertaining, and very humorous.

Cindy is a successful real estate agent, mother of three, and is a member of several organizations in the community. She loves her job and how it allows her to meet and interact with lots of new people. She loves to chat with prospects, and it is not rare that she'll end up befriending them, regardless whether they buy from her or not.
She attributes her success in business to her openness, honesty, and enthusiasm she displays during the sales process. Actually…, she does not like to think of it as "sales process" – she thinks of it as "helping people find their dream home" (or the one they can afford).
Everyday, she tries to leave her office before 5:30, but she regularly stays late. The reasons for this are various: she has to catch up with paperwork (something that she always tends to be behind with), meeting prospects who can't meet her early in the day), and often she simply loses track of time.
At home she tries to be the best mother and wife possible. She is playing with her kids almost daily and gets her regular exercise by riding the bike with the kids, jumping with them on the trampoline, and by doing other outdoor various fun activities.
She at times feels guilty for spending too much time away from the kids, involved in different types of organizations: PTO (parent teacher organization), SIC(school improvement council), Toastmasters (improve public speaking), Rotary Club, and Chamber of Commerce. She loves to attend these meetings where she can socialize with her "friends" and prospects; as well as she sees it as an integral part of being a business person. She believes that regular and effective networking is one of the main keys to her success.

---

[1] - not her real name

Her husband – with who she has a great relationship - often accuses her of being air headed. She often has to turn back from the street to get her bag or other things, and often leaves things at home and has to drive back later to get them (or gets in some trouble for noticing too late that she doesn't have them). She at times misses appointments due to forgetting to look in her planner; or totally forgets to transfer the meeting date and time into her planner from the piece of paper she jotted the information down on and shuffled in her pocket or purse.

While she is content with the level of professional success she is experiencing, she knows she could be much more successful if she became more organized and focused.

Cindy is a great example of a **high** I style individual.

Communication Style

- ☑ high I style individuals tend to be very perceptive of other's emotions and will often offer help, support, and/or a listening ear
- ☑ are fast paced talkers
- ☑ use lots of humor
- ☑ like telling stories (and jokes)
- ☑ they tend to speak with enthusiasm, often with a radiant face and an almost constant smile
- ☑ often make their points through stories
- ☑ have difficulty giving brief answers
- ☑ they first talk and then think
- ☑ they unintentionally hurt other people's feelings occasionally, by saying things that they did not think through before speaking
- ☑ they tend to be extroverts who often share information that others can perceive as inappropriate or offensive
- ☑ they are great networkers – they love to meet and socialize with many different types of people
- ☑ they'll usually try to avoid conflict; but also tremendously enjoy good verbal duels where they can use their persuasive and influencing skills to win over their "opponents"

- ☑ they are great at generating new ideas (though not always so great at implementing them)
- ☑ they are more interested in big-picture conversations, rather than in-depth detail or technically oriented conversations
- ☑ when in team environment – or when catching others in a conflict situation – they get a kick out of trying to play the peace-maker (which they usually accomplish rather successfully). They often accomplish this by downplaying the importance of the topic of the argument, and other times they simply help the arguing parties calm down and discuss the topic in a more civilized manner. Occasionally their intervention creates a larger conflict, in which case they feel extremely frustrated.
- ☑ they often have strong opinions and like to persuade others – occasionally even through heated debate - to accept those opinions
- ☑ are open to listening to others' opinions and even solicit others' input; but they are not always patient enough to listen till the other person is done talking
- ☑ they are people-pleasers who crave very much for acceptance, which often makes them be way too agreeable and diminishes their assertiveness
- ☑ they love to praise others and celebrate others' successes
- ☑ they can use their verbal skills to gain approval and popularity (they fear social rejection and will do anything to avoid it)
- ☑ when they explain something, they want to make sure that others understand exactly what they are trying to get across; therefore, they often over explain things
- ☑ since they like to be the center of attention, they tend to speak and laugh loudly (most often this is not even a conscious choice for most I style individuals, they are just naturally wired this way)
- ☑ they are an open book, expressing openly their emotions and feelings
- ☑ they are quick to strike conversations with total strangers and easily form new friendships
- ☑ quick to anger; quick to calm down; quick to forgive and forget

Strengths and Weaknesses

Here are some of the strengths of I style individuals:

- ☑ easy to get along with
- ☑ great at defusing tensed situations with humor, stories, or other quick witty intervention
- ☑ welcomes changes and adapts to them easily
- ☑ quick decision maker
- ☑ open to new ideas
- ☑ open to try out new experiences
- ☑ has a positive outlook in life; is great at finding the good in most situations
- ☑ great at seeing the good in everyone around them
- ☑ looks for ways to improve her own life and others' lives
- ☑ are great at improving coworkers' and team morale
- ☑ is great at creating enthusiasm and sell an idea to team members (or to total strangers)
- ☑ can easily come up with creative ways to entertain self and others
- ☑ great at networking and entertaining people of all backgrounds
- ☑ works well with others
- ☑ very comfortable around total strangers – loves meeting new people - and strikes up conversations easily, often chatting in minutes as if they'd known each other for years
- ☑ tends to be very accepting with everyone around them (though, they do wish that some people around them smiled more, and they will try to liven up these "fun-busters")
- ☑ they are expressive – everyone knows exactly what they think and how they feel
- ☑ they are good at inspiring others

It is important to note that each style's "strengths" are truly strengths when used in moderation. As uncle Ben said in the movie *Spiderman* "With great powers come great responsibilities" – and the same applies to each style's strengths…

- ☑ they are almost constantly enthusiastic about something; their enthusiasm is often "contagious," helping others see new possibilities, feel hope, or see certain things in more positive ways
- ☑ easy to anger but quick to calm down; they forgive quickly as well and tend to forget negative events
- ☑ able to respond quickly to the demands of her environment, adapting smoothly to new situations
- ☑ is usually charismatic and well-liked
- ☑ usually has a wide network of friends and business acquaintances
- ☑ loves to help others
- ☑ great at defusing tensed situations or conflicts
- ☑ praises everything: the weather, new furniture, others' accomplishments, efforts, attire, hairdo, etc. - anything that attracts their eyes
- ☑ helps others through introducing them to the appropriate person in their vast circle of "friends"
- ☑ comes across as a happy and fulfilled person

It is important to note that each style's "strengths" are truly strengths when used in moderation. As uncle Ben said in the movie *Spiderman* "With great powers come great responsibilities" – and the same applies to each style's strengths. Our strengths are perceived as such only when we keep them under control (or when used responsibly, to use uncle Ben's term). Out of control, regardless of what style one might be, our strengths become weaknesses.

> Your *weaknesses* are often the result of allowing your *strengths* to be pushed to extreme.

Here's a list of some of the I style individuals' strengths that turn into weaknesses when pushed to the extreme or get out of control:

Strengths Under Control	Strengths Out of Control
Communicative	*Becomes Defensive / Boastful / Attacks Verbally / Gossipy*
People Oriented	*Disorganized / Forgetful*
Caring	*Prying / Intrusive / Emotional*
Entertaining	*Annoying / Interrupts Others / Show-off*
Friendly	
Humorous	
Helpful	*Over-Promising / Pushy / Irritating*
Enthusiastic	*Annoying / Impulsive*
Fun-Loving	*Careless / Sloppy / Unsystematic / Scatterbrained*
Curious	*Easily Distracted*
Interested	
Independent	*Lost / Undisciplined / Lacks Purpose & Direction*
Creative	*Unrealistic / Inconsistent / Scatter-minded*
Innovative	
Compassionate	*Easy target / Sucker / Permissive*
Optimistic	
People Pleaser	
Outgoing	*Reckless / Irresponsible*
Persuasive	*Pushy / Irritating*
Smiling & Kind	*Fake*
Spontaneous	*Impulsive/Unpredictable*

Table 5.1 – Influence Style: Strengths become weaknesses when pushed to extremes

Challenge Areas

As one reads about the gregarious, outgoing, sociable Influence style, one almost gets to wonder if they also have super-natural powers. Of course, they have only as many supernatural powers as you or I, but they often behave as they were some superheroes ready to jump into rescuing anyone in need.

But with all this enthusiasm and "super" qualities, they too have several challenge areas:

- Like D's, I style individuals are also often poor listeners. I style individuals have soooo much to share and never enough people to listen to them. God/nature gave us two ears and one mouth; that should be a reminder to both the D and the I styles that they should listen twice as much as they talk.
- They have selective hearing – they only hear what they want to hear OR what they are tuned in to hear. When they listen to a long message, training, etc., they tune in and out and only hear part of what is being said.
- They easily lose track of time when chatting with someone. Often their paperwork or other technical projects get left for the last moment due to excessive socializing.
- Has   poor   concept   of time
  - is regularly late from meetings and other appointments
  - at times will show up on the wrong day for appointments
  - often underestimates (and at times overestimates) required time for task-completion
  - gets lost in conversations, totally oblivious to how much time is trickling away
- Often lacks clear goals and priorities; tends to approach tasks at random
- They can get lost in being busy, and feeling productive, performing lengthy processes, vs. completing tasks and moving towards a definite objective (for example, designing a simple flyer or a brochure can take them days, or weeks, at times; they get absorbed in picking the right color, right shapes, etc., only to change their minds and start the process all over)
- They don't mind working individually on hands-on activities for short periods of time, , but have to regularly follow up on them. They tend to procrastinate and are poor at following through with their plans (given that they had a plan to start with)

- High I style individuals love to take action but get easily bored with tasks that take too long to complete, require too much detail work, or does not give them a chance to interact with others throughout the process.
- At times they will display more confidence than what they can back up with real life experience or knowledge. They might not always be aware of their limitations.
- Because of the I's tendency to task-hop, procrastinate, AND their tendency to get excited about new things (and bored with the existing ones), they often end up giving up on long or complex projects; or they'll complete them at the last minute (often with several errors).
- Tends to solve problems through impulsively trying out different solutions (trial-and-error "method"), vs. careful planning and thinking through possible solutions
- I style individuals tend to speak in superlatives. Whatever they experience now, is the *best ever, most delicious, most beautiful,* etc.
- They love to praise others, but they often over do it and others are unsure how sincere is the praise they get
- They tend to exaggerate when retelling an event (if they saw three swans at the lake, they'll tell you they saw about seven swans)
- They like to daydream – occasionally can daydream in the midst of a meeting, during a conversation, or while working, totally tuning out of what's going on around them (can erroneously be identified as having ADD)
- Are excitable – they get attracted to new ideas and will jump into new things/projects impulsively... only to get excited about something else down the road (at times after a few hours or days) and jump into the new thing with the same enthusiasm and abandoning the previous project. This "process" can be repeated at regular intervals and many of the projects they start will never get finished.
- They often try to soften or downplay the gravity or importance of negative information/negative situation
- They are great at intervening and breaking up others' arguments; however, most often will leave the issues unresolved, focusing exclusively on calming the arguing parties down
- They are people pleasers who tend to avoid conflict (often) at all cost; because of this, they sometimes settle for lose-win outcomes.

- Under pressure or during conflict, will openly express emotions and can resort to verbal attacks
- While they seem really brave and confident, when conflict arises they often fail to be assertive and fail to openly speak up on what bothers them (especially when they feel disrespected or treated unjustly)
- Due to their optimism and acceptance of others, they at times might get taken advantage off; or get ripped off rather easily. Experience often helps them get better with time in this area.
- Can be overly permissive, which can backfire if you are a manager or parent
- They have difficulty working side-by-side with quiet, introvert, or no-communicative individuals (C style or CD style). They feel NOT liked and this causes them to feel constantly stressed.

Knowledge is Power! Take control of your weaknesses!

Nobody is perfect, except me.

I style individuals often believe that everyone should be just like them: outgoing, smiling, friendly, and just simply happy-go-lucky all the time. After all, wouldn't this be a better world if everyone was an I style?

Well, the I styles might think so, but we know better, right? If everyone was an I style, we'd spend our days chatting away and having fun all the time and no one would get anything done.

Just like any of the other three styles, I style individuals have their blind spots – areas that they can take some effort to improve upon. And as I mentioned earlier, most of our weaknesses are simply the result of abusing our strengths. Often all we have to do is take control of our strengths in order to become more effective at communicating with those around us and accomplishing goals more effectively.

Understand that most of your strengths – fast paced, communicative, spontaneous, humorous, friendly, etc. - are your best allies in creating and maintaining great relationships; but at the same time, occasionally they can be the very traits that can make you less effective in accomplishing personal and professional goals. Also, when you overuse these strengths, they can be detrimental to your relationships as well.

Read carefully the following suggestions and consider implementing the ones that you feel will aid you in becoming more productive and better at maintaining successful relationships with those around you:

- Use a planner! If you are a high I, you probably have difficulty remembering many of the things you commit to and you'll greatly benefit from developing the habit of using a planner to record appointments, deadlines, goals, ideas, etc.
- Try NOT to promise more than what you can handle! Again, your planner should be a great help to stay on track with what you can and cannot do. Instead of saying yes to everything, let the other party know that you'll get back to them after you check your planner.
- In meetings, training, or during other important events, get in the habit of taking notes AND reading your notes later.
- When you are unsure about something, ask someone who knows, vs. becoming "creative" and making it up as you go.
- Eliminate task-hopping (nope, it is not a sport)! Set goals and sub-goals. Break down your goals in manageable short-term goals and work on one (but no more than three) sub-goal(s) at a time and stay focused on those till you finish them. (You've already noticed that task-hopping often results in not accomplishing anything; it's perhaps time to try a new approach)
- Take time to think of possible consequences before you take a major decision (I styles tend to make decisions impulsively)
- You often read people's emotions very accurately and sense when something is not right; however, be careful not to pry. Learn who welcomes your help and who prefers not to be bothered.
- One of your greatest strengths is your enthusiasm and your beautiful smiling face; but be careful not to overdo it on the job. Some of the other styles do not understand how someone can be so upbeat all the time and will think that you are faking it, and some can get annoyed by your constant upbeat attitude. **Solution1**: on the job, tone it down a bit. Try to reach into your D and C style behaviors and be more on-the-task type guy – at least for parts of the day. In the long-run it'll be beneficial for everyone.
  Solution2: if it's clear that your environment appreciates you as you are – or if you work directly with clients and you've accomplished considerable success with your current approach, then fire away and stay true to who you are (do understand

though that some of your clients/customers and coworkers would want to be treated more along the lines of their styles: be more serious, brief and to the point with the Ds and the Cs, and be considerate, kind, and supportive with the Ss).

- Do not allow others to take advantage of your "sunny" and agreeable nature. If you feel that someone is trying to pull a "funny" on you, reach into your D style (trust me, it's in there) and let them know how you feel; verbalize your sense that the deal feels somewhat (or very) unfair.
  I (and S) style individuals will often accept a deal, even if it's clearly unfavorable to them, just not to upset the other person or to avoid possible conflict.
- Remember, rules were made to be followed (yes, by everyone – even you). Of course, it is easier to follow them if you know about them, right? (Often I style individuals bend or break rules because they don't even know about the existence of some of the rules and procedures they are supposed to follow)
- Interacting with others is fun as well as often important to your success on your job, but getting organized and staying organized is often equally important. Learn some organizational skills and you'll be surprised to see your effectiveness quadruple. If possible, take a *How to Get and Stay Organized* class.
- Interacting with others is fun, but when overdone it will considerably diminish your productivity. Develop some techniques to keep your non-job related chats short: stand up when you speak with someone, walk towards the door (after a while), take a peak at your watch regularly, let them know that you have a deadline to meet, etc.
- Try to use superlatives sparingly! "It's been the <u>best</u> movie I've ever seen!"; "It was the <u>most </u>delicious frog-more-stew ever!" "It was the <u>hardest</u> thing I ever had to do"…
  While for you, in the moment, it might feel like the best or worst food, movie, etc., if you overdo your superlatives, soon those around you will not take you seriously. So, use your **extreme** praise and criticism sparingly.
- Break the habit of agreeing instantly with everyone! I style individuals tend to be people-pleasers and will agree with most things they hear (or instantly disagree, if it's totally against their beliefs). However, if you keep being agreeable all the time, it will be hard for others to take your opinions seriously.
- Try not to dismiss or disagree instantly with whatever seems **not** right to you. Just because the immediate appearance of an idea is wrong, it is not sure it's wrong. One way to get to the bottom

of it is by saying "Let me see if I understand what you are saying…" and you repeat the core of what you just heard. If the other party agrees and says that you heard it correctly, then you could say "To me this seems unreasonable / unbelievable /unrealistic / totally nuts /etc." (Instead of saying "This is bull manure!" you let the other party know that to you this seems out of whack.) Not everything is black or white – just because to you something seems not right, it does not mean it is not so. Besides, there are many instances when both parties are 100% right, they just fail to notice it.

- Listen with an open mind to criticism – or feedback – of your work or your actions, and instead of becoming defensive, discuss how you can improve
- Control your tendency to brag about your accomplishments or super abilities. While it is fun for you to share, it can get annoying, after a while, to listen to "how great you are."
- Control your tendency to exaggerate. Try to gain attention through real accomplishment (which probably you have plenty), vs. "adding a bit" to your accomplishments or experiences to make things more interesting.
- Try not to gossip – you can lose many friends and gain many enemies that way
- Practice verbalizing your frustrations and dislikes with coworkers and supervisors – do it in a polite but assertive way (reach into your D style behaviors). In a conflict situation, it is ok to stop smiling, take a deep breath, and calmly let the other person know what's bothering you.
- Make a conscious effort to slow down and listen to those around you – that is really listen[1] - and make your conversations less about you and your experiences, and more about the issues that are being discussed
- Occasionally, allow others to "shine" – sit back and enjoy your friends, family, or coworkers and control your urge to set the tone, entertain everyone, or otherwise control the outcome of the moment. They say that everyone has their five minutes of fame – (occasionally) allow those around you to have their five minutes of fame.
- Commit to spend some time with a high C style individual on a regular basis and try to adapt your behaviors to her expectations. Listen well, talk only when you know what you are talking

---

[1] - See pg. 42, *Effective Communication Starts with Effective Listening,* for more on listening skills

about, slow down, be patient, ask questions and listen to the full answers... And study your C style "friend," see what you can learn from her. How does she stay organized, how does she accomplish goals, etc.

- Capitalize on your strengths and you'll be viewed as an influential personality; allow your strengths to get out of control, and you'll be viewed as a chaotic clown.

And...

- Change your car's oil as required and check the oil level and your tire air pressure at least once a month – you don't want to be one of those people whose car stops in the middle of nowhere because you never change your oil and your engine dies on you
- Tune up your lawn mower at least once a year
- Schedule regular maintenance for your computer (weekly is best, but at least monthly). I know it tests your patience when your computer is slow – you can avoid this by giving it a few minutes of your time once in a while.

Remember!

Each of the four sets of behaviors are available to you!

Just like when having access to four bowls of fruits, you might prefer one fruit over the other, but it is up to you to reach in one or the other bowl and consume any of the four fruits.

The same applies to the four behavioral styles(D, I, S, and C). They are at your fingertips at all times and it is up to you to borrow behaviors from any of them to make you more effective in any social situation. It might not always feel very comfortable or natural[1], but it is the most effective way to creating and maintaining successful relationships.

---

[1] - **D**'s have difficulty slowing down and listening well; I styles often have difficulty being bottom-line in delivering information; S styles often find it hard to be assertive and direct; and **C**s at times find it difficult to loosen up and socialize freely (smiling, not judging, sharing own stories, etc.) – when raising our awareness of these blind spots, we can take a conscious effort to address them.

Expectations of Others

Here's what most I style individuals would say, if they had a chance to express freely their expectations of those around them:

- *When I talk to you – or you talk to me – please smile and look me in the eyes*
- *If you have a problem with me, let's discuss it openly. Do not yell at me or lecture me.* (They want to shine – they want to be the best at what they do, hence they appreciate any feedback and will try to do better in the future. They do not respond well to formal warnings or loud lecturing.)
- *Share with me your stories and, if possible, use humor in your conversation*
- *Listen to my stories and jokes <u>and</u> laugh with me*
- *When working on a project, let's discuss thoroughly the steps that we need to take and how we'll go about completing those steps* (I style individuals usually learn best by doing and/or by observing others)
- *Be upbeat and conversational throughout the day* (if you tend to be more introvert, the I style individual can take it personally and thinks you don't like him or   her; they will try for a while to get you involved in regular light conversation, and if they keep failing, they can get really frustrated and stressed)
- *When you see I'm doing something right, do praise me. I love to get recognition for my efforts.*

When their expectations are not met, I style individuals can become frustrated with those around them. Just like every other style, they believe that everyone else should be just like them (friendly, communicative, helpful, humorous, enthusiastic, etc).

The I style – as each of the other styles, as well – will benefit tremendously from learning about and understanding the diverse nature of different behavioral styles. This knowledge will improve the I style's acceptance levels of others, letting them understand that the people around them are not there to stress them; nor can they reasonably expect everyone to act the way the I styles naturally act, and will understand that "different" means "different," NOT "difficult."

How to Deal with Conflict when Dealing with an I Style Individual

- Listen to his side of the story
- Validate his feelings (say "I understand how this can make you sad/angry.") Remember, I style individuals are very much in touch with their feelings, hence this step is crucial in effectively resolving a conflict with an **I**.
- Praise their strengths – or some recent positive accomplishment - before discussing the conflicting issue. If you leave out this step, they'll get really devastated and can get verbally aggressive or overly defensive. It is easier to get them to listen and cooperate if you first acknowledge some of their strengths.
- Stress that this discussion is not about him personally, but about a specific issue that needs a solution; attempt to get him to try to figure out – or figure out together - how to solve the problem in most effective manner.
- Try to steer the conversation on specific facts (and away from discussing emotions and feelings) by using questions requiring specific answers, such as *when, where, what, who,* and *how.*
- When reaching a consensus, ask him to repeat what you agreed about (to ensure that he really heard you well and that you both reached the same conclusion)
- If you are in management position, ask for a commitment regarding the steps to be taken to correct the issue of the discussion
- Reinforce your confidence in him – let him leave with the feeling that you trust and believe in him
- At times an I style individual might not even be aware of the existence of a problem (due to their optimistic and accepting nature). In this case explain the problem and the potential consequences that can develop in case the problem is not taken care of.
- If in order to resolve the conflict the I style person needs to complete some technical task, provide some very specific guidance, listen to what steps they plan to take in order to rectify the problem, and possibly even assign a helper. Follow up on his progress and be encouraging and supportive.

Remember!

In conflict, the truth is rarely "black" or "white" – more often then not both of you might be right; you just have to be willing to take time to understand each other's point of view and...
1. agree to disagree agreeably, or
2. come to the realization that the issue at hand can be viewed in multiple ways and you are both right, or
3. come up with a happy medium (compromise), or
4. synergize: come up with a third, better option; a solution that will satisfy both of you.

Influence Style - The Source of Joy and Inspiration

It is not uncommon to hear others call I styles a *show off, he thinks he's the center of the universe, clown,* and other creative descriptors to describe this high-spirited and lively behavioral style...

Call them what you want, fact is that as the sun is the source of the light for our planet, I style individuals are without any doubt the life of every party, household, and workplace. They are the ones who when they step into a room, it feels as if someone had turned the *light* of fun and ecstasy on. With their quick wit, confidence, humorous stories, and loud funny comments, they liven up everyone, no matter what your original mood was. And while some think that I style individuals consciously try to be in the spotlight wherever they go, the truth is they do not have to try at all – it all comes naturally. Most of them, in fact, learn to tone it down to avoid being perceived as a clown or unserious.

I style individuals are naturally optimistic and tend to see the humorous part of mostly anything and everything around them. Through their enthusiasm, confidence, and charisma, they often successfully influence others' moods and decisions. No matter the bad mood someone is experiencing, once an I style colleague, family member, or friend shows up, the person will get cheered up in minutes. (Except **perhaps** if the person with the dark mood is a high C style individual, who might get more annoyed by the I style's bouncing-off-the-walls attitude.)

They are also natural at praising others' accomplishments or whatever attracts their eyes. They tend to see the best in people and will openly express their good impression; they also tend to see the best in every situation. Whether at a party or in a crowded elevator, I style individuals always have something nice to say... Yes, even to total strangers.

They perform great in any position that require constant interaction, such as trainers, public speakers, teachers, etc[1].

Of course, as I stated earlier, anyone can reach into their I style behaviors and choose to be personable, enthusiastic, and entertaining. We all have met S, C, and D behavioral style individuals who regularly display I style behaviors. Anyone can chose to be sociable and caring – it is a question of will and motivation. It might not come naturally at first, but it's being done everyday and there's no magic to it. The more you practice it the easier it gets.

To be most effective in social situations, it is really important to learn a few lessons from high I style individuals. Of course, not all social situations require outrageous humor or wit. You definitely don't want to reach in your I style behaviors during a funeral or other serious social gathering. But you will definitely be a more effective manager, coworker, parent, and friend, if you learn to regularly view the light side of life once in a while, and learn to loosen up.

How to Motivate the I Style Individual

Regardless whether we are talking about an employee, child, a spouse, or significant other, there are a few simple ways to motivate these passionate and expressive individuals. While many of the suggestions below apply to motivating employees, there are also some that can be equally applied in other types of relationships.

- Let them work at their own pace (while making sure to set very specific deadlines)
- Give instructions in writing (this will avoid the "I forgot" or the "I didn't hear it" excuse)
- "I know you can do it! I've seen in the past what you are capable of," and similar statements are the igniting words to set the I type on the go. They crave recognition and success, and when they

---

[1] - See pg. 149 for more careers I style individuals tend to enjoy and be successful at

hear that someone believes in them, they want to prove them right. They also love to shine and be the center of attention; therefore the accomplishment of a new task that puts them in the spotlight is appealing to them.

- "It will be fun!" "Have some fun with it!" "Make me proud!" The words *fun, proud, exciting,* and other fun- or prestige-oriented words, always make the I style want to do well.
- Provide them opportunities to use their verbal skills
- Capitalize on their desire for public recognition – I style individuals are probably the easiest to reward for their efforts. They are probably the only style that gets real satisfaction from being praised in front of their pears. An *Employee of the Year (or Month), Salesperson of the year (or Month),* or other fancy certificate delivered to them at a formal or semi-formal event, will make them as happy as one can be. They will try to achieve those titles year after year and will display them proudly on the walls of their office.

  (Some of the other styles – especially the D and the C might shove them in a box or a bottom drawer and mumble that "a little bonus would have been more appropriate.." S style individuals love to be recognized for their efforts and will highly appreciate a certificate of accomplishment, however, they do not enjoy being in the spotlight when receiving the award.)
- While they crave public recognition, they are also highly motivated by monetary rewards (especially when they feel they added considerably to the bottom line)

Remember!
Motivating others can be "tricky." You can ONLY motivate people to do things they are interested in. Trying to motivate different styles to complete tasks that are against their natural behavioral tendencies can be futile and ineffective. Take the effort to recognize the behavioral style of the person who you are working with and motivate them by allowing them to capitalize on their natural strengths[1].

---

[1] - Have your employee(s) take a DiSC® PPSS (or DiSC 2.0) to ensure that you get an accurate reading of the person's behavioral style. The DiSC profile will also suggest ways to motivate the person most effectively – for more details and to see a sample profile, visit **www.egSebastian.com/assessments**

What Demotivates I Style Individuals

- Lack of opportunities to "show off" their skills; more exactly, lack of opportunity to use their verbal skills to solve problems or defuse conflict, interact with clients, work on gaining new clients, teach others new skills, influence others, entertain, or otherwise utilize their verbal skills
- A micro-managing manager or supervisor
- Needing to report on every move they make
- Feeling disrespected by superiors or coworkers
- Lack of opportunities for interaction
- Monotonous work
- Heavily analytical and technical work

I Style Most Popular Career Choices[1]

Table 4.2 – I Style Most Popular Career Choices

Actor	Announcer	Athlete
Advertising Manager*	Instructional Coordinator***	Insurance Sales Agent
Meeting and Convention Planner* + ***	Customer Service Manager*	Commercial and Industrial Designer***
Counselor**	Cashier	Clergy** + ***
Choreographer***	Childcare Worker**	Interviewer* or ****
Dancer	Entrepreneur*	Courier
Farmer and Rancher	Firefighter*	Correspondent*
Musicians	Marketing Manager*	Sales Representative
Journalist	Photo Journalist	Rock Star*
Public Speaker*	Personnel Recruiter*	Real Estate Broker
Photographer	Property Manager*	Product Promoter
Public Relations Specialist	Talk Show and Other Show Host	Promotions Manager*
Public Relations Manager*	Teacher Assistant**	Recreational Therapist**
Receptionist**	Recreation Worker	Reporter*
Purchasing Agent*	Retail Salesperson	Professional Athlete
Real Estate Manager*	Sales Manager*	Stuntman*
Social Worker**	Stand-up Comedian	Social Worker*
Animal Care and Service Worker*	Customer Service Representative	Trainer & Workshop Presenter
Travel Agent**	Travel Clerk*	Teacher*
Real Estate Agent	Taxi Driver	Youth Counselors*

* - often in ID combination
** - often in IS combination
*** often in IC or ISC combination
**** often in IDC combination

These are only a few of the careers most I style individuals tend to enjoy due to the many opportunities where they can use their verbal skills and satisfy their need to be in social settings.

If your behavioral style blend contains two (or three) styles at about the same intensity[1] levels, remember to check the most popular career choices for your secondary style as well. If, for example, you are an ID style individual, you'll probably enjoy several of the careers listed in the *D's Most Popular Career Choices* on page 117.

Power Tip #5

Hold I styles accountable to their commitments!

I style individuals are very enthusiastic and quick to offer help, often taking on more than they can realistically accomplish. Unfortunately, they are quick at promising to do something, but often as quick at forgetting it or procrastinating on tasks.

Help them be the success they mean to be by reminding them their commitment(s) and holding them accountable to them. A simple way to do this is by helping them develop intermediate goals and checking up on them regularly to see how the accomplishment of the intermediate goals come along.

Caution! Check on the accomplishment of the intermediate goals vs. asking about them. I styles at times are quick at answering with a "creative" fib, thinking that they'll complete the task later in the day or "first thing in the morning." Unfortunately, they often forget about it and the task never gets completed or gets completed in the last moment, somewhat on the sloppy side.

---

[1] To get an accurate idea of what is your behavioral style, complete the valid and reliable DiSC® 2.0, DiSC 2Plus, or DiSC PPSS profile, at **www.egsebastian.com/disc_classic**

Influence Style: *Improve Your Relationships and Effectiveness* **Self-Coaching Worksheet**
(Print out a blank self-coaching sheet at **www.egSebastian.com/SelfCoach**)

1. What are my strengths that I'm most proud of?

_____

_____

_____

2. What are some of my strengths that make me most effective in my
environment?

_____

_____

_____

3. What are some of my strengths that are (perhaps) perceived as
weaknesses in my environment?

_____

_____

_____

4. What are some of my weaknesses that make me less effective in my
environment?

_____

_____

_____

5. Based on what I read in this chapter (and on what I already knew),
what can I do to become more effective at creating and maintaining
successful relationships in my workplace and/or at home? (Pages 138 -
142)

_____

_____

_____

6. Based on what I read in this chapter (and on what I already knew), what can I do to become more effective at setting and accomplishing personal and professional goals? (Pages 138 -142)

_____

_____

_____

_____

_____

_____

_____

_____

7. Is it an option to speak to my supervisor (or coworkers) and ask to be assigned tasks that are more in line with my strengths? If yes, how would I approach him/her/them about it?

_____

_____

_____

_____

8. What else can I do to become more effective in all areas of my life? (Based on what you read – e.g., talk to spouse or significant other about your style and your style's needs, behavioral tendencies; how can you improve your relationship with loved ones, etc.)

_____

_____

_____

_____

_____

_____

_____

154

Remember!
<u>No behavioral style is better or worse</u>! Each and every style has its strengths and weaknesses.   You can become the "best you" when you get a good understanding of your style, learn to capitalize on your strengths, and – if you choose to – work on some of your weak areas.   You are already perfect as you are – you just have to use your gifts to your advantage.

Chapter 6

The Steadiness Style

> The Steadiness (S) Style – Quick Overview
> How to Easily Recognize an S Style Individual
> Friendly and Efficient Julia
> Communication Style
> Strengths and Weaknesses
> Challenge Areas
> Knowledge is Power! Take control of your weaknesses!
> Expectations of Others
> How to Deal with Conflict when Dealing with an S Style Individual
> Steadiness Style – the "Real Best Friend"
> How to Motivate the S Style Individual
> What Demotivates the S Style Individual
> S's Most Popular Career Choices
> Power Tip #6: *Be patient and gentle with the S styles around you!*
> Steadiness Style: Self-Coaching Worksheet

Famous High S Examples:

- Mahatma Gandhi
- Barbara Bush
- John Denver (SI)
- Forest Whitaker (SC)
- Meg Ryan
- Tom Brokaw
- President Jimmy Carter

The Steadiness (S) Style – Quick Overview

Steadiness (S) – moderate paced **and** *people oriented*
S's are calm and kind people, who are great at giving support and comfort to others, follow rules, are great listeners and are great team players.

☑ Do you tend to move and talk at a more moderate pace?

☑ Do you prefer working around friendly, supportive, and peaceful people?

☑ Do you tend to be calm, friendly, and supportive with those around you?

☑ Do you tend to naturally smile whenever someone approaches you?

☑ Do you tend to take your time to make good decisions?

☑ Do you tend to be cautious – or at times hesitant - when faced with unknown situations (on the job or in your personal life)?

☑ Are you most of the time a great listener?

☑ Do you enjoy comforting and helping others?

☑ Do you dislike sudden changes that affect your routine at work or at home?

☑ Would you describe yourself as humble and easygoing?

If you answered "yes" to most of these questions, then you most likely are a high S –Steadiness - style[1] individual, or a combination of two or more styles with some high S style traits.

Or perhaps you know someone in your environment who fits this description. If yes, it is most likely that this person is an S style individual and displays most of the behaviors described in this chapter.

---

[1]To get an accurate idea of what is your behavioral style, complete the valid and reliable DiSC® 2.0, DiSC 2Plus, or DiSC PPSS profile, at **www.egsebastian.com/disc_classic**

Figure 6.1 – S style individuals often come across as calm, content, and as greatest listeners

S style individuals are most easily recognized by noticing who in your environment tends to consistently come across as calm, friendly, and content, while approaching people (and life in general) with a loving, warm smile.

When you step into the office of an S style, or visit them in their home, you'll notice lots of family pictures, little trays with candy or other type of treats, perhaps a mini water fountain....

Approximate percentage of high S style individuals in the US:

Men - 23%

Women 31%

They love to create a feel of home-like environment regardless where they are.

S style individuals are the ones who most of us instinctively tend to approach whenever we need to pour out our hearts. They are naturally great listeners – the best of the four styles –are very considerate of others feelings and emotions, and derive great enjoyment from helping others

Because of their friendly and supportive nature, S style individuals are at times easily manipulated by others; however, once they gain awareness of this, many S style individuals successfully put a stop to it, which often is as simple as learning to say the magical two-letter word "NO[1]."

Individuals who are more moderate paced – both in their rate of speech and physical movement - AND are more interested in being around (and working with) people, tend to adopt mostly behaviors from the Steadiness set of behaviors (pg. 159) and we call them Steadiness (S) Style individuals.

This chapter is dedicated to describing in detail the behavioral tendencies of Steadiness (S) style individuals.

Remember!
<u>No behavioral style is better or worse!</u> Each and every style has its strengths and weaknesses. You can become the "best you" when you get a good understanding of your style, learn to capitalize on your strengths, and – if you choose to – work on some of your weak areas. You are already perfect as you are – you just have to use your gifts to your advantage.

---

[1] - See Appendix C, on page 252 for more on how to say "No" without feeling that you are offending others

The Steadiness (S) Behavioral Style

Influence style individuals tend to consistently adopt **most** of the following behaviors:

General Tendencies:
- ☑ Tends to talk and move at a more moderate pace
- ☑ Believes rules were made to be followed
- ☑ Respects and follows traditions
- ☑ Does not mind performing routine tasks
- ☑ Is (usually) great at finishing what she starts
- ☑ Likes to know her exact job duties/description and will follow it as closely as possible
- ☑ Prefers working with people vs. working with tasks, numbers, or concepts
- ☑ Kind, helpful, and sociable
- ☑ Likes peace and friendly people.

Communication Style:
- ☑ Moderate paced and calm
- ☑ The best listener of the four styles
- ☑ Tries to avoid conflict at all cost
- ☑ Doesn't like to be rushed
- ☑ Has difficulty saying "NO"
- ☑ Tends to NOT express resentments and hurts
- ☑ Is considerate; tries not to hurt others feelings
- ☑ Can become emotional
- ☑ Often will hide negative emotions in order to avoid conflict
- ☑ Is kind and respectful with everyone around them

S Style Motto:
- ☑ Let's be friendly and patient with one another and let's make things work through team effort!

I heard someone once say that "Steadiness style people are the teddy bears of the human zoo," and I couldn't agree more with that comment. S style individuals are the sweetest, kindest, and the easiest to get along with.

Their love for people and consideration of others' feelings makes it hard for them to be antagonistic or openly critical of others; therefore they'll do everything possible to avoid any kind of conflict or disagreements. They often control their emotions and will not express resentment or dislike even when someone offends them face-to-face.

In romantic relationships, they are the easiest to love, due to their sweet easygoing nature, and their constant focus on making sure that both parties in the relationship are happy.

At work they are highly dependable and they will finish what they start (though at a considerable slower pace than a D or I style manager or coworker would expect). They are always available to help their coworkers in any way they can; as well as are always available to listen to others' problems or complaints.

They love predictability in their days and do not mind routine tasks, as long as they can work at their own pace, are around people, and feel appreciated. Unfortunately some S style individuals get stuck in their routine activities and get to believe that they are doing a great job fulfilling those tasks. In certain environments this can be effective (e.g. counselors, social workers, teachers, etc.), but can come across as having lack of initiative, slow, or even lazy at times in faster paced environments, especially where job descriptions are not very clear cut.

When they capitalize on their strengths – or allowed to capitalize on their strengths - S style individuals are the most reliable and sociable individuals that we'll ever meet; when, however, they abuse their strengths, they will come across as slowpokes and/or an obstacle to progress and change.

When a person tends to adopt mostly behaviors from the Steadiness (S) style set of behaviors on a consistent basis, this person would be called a
S Style individual
(or Steadiness Style Individual)

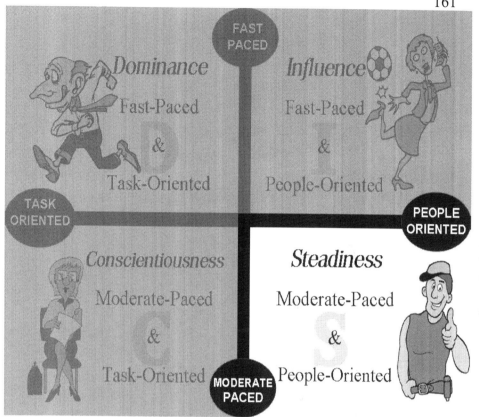

Figure 6.2 – The Steadiness Style: Moderate Paced & People Oriented

How to Easily Recognize an S Style Individual

While most of us are a combination of two or more styles, most of us have a dominant style which is rather easy to spot.

S style individuals are easily recognized by noticing their more moderate pace - both in their rate of speech and physical movement - combined with a genuine interest and love for people (Fig. 6.2). They are easygoing, humble, and dependable people who like to do things (work or other tasks) at a steady pace without being rushed.

Friendly and Efficient Julia

It's Tuesday, and it's Julia's[1] off day. She's an RN who works 12-hour shifts, working two nights straight and then having two nights off. It can get tiring at times, but she loves her job dearly.

On her days off, when she's done with her house chores; she likes to go to shop or just brows clothing stores. On these shopping trips, there are probably very few times when she is not recognized by other shoppers. They come up to her and give her a BiiiiG hug, which she gladly returns with a great smile and with emotions running high. These people are past patients or family members of past patients.

Julia regularly gets small gifts and lots of thank-you cards from her patients, as well as she gets invited to visit the home of some, after they leave the hospital. She has been chosen employee of the months many times due to the feedback the patients leave behind as they leave.

While she really loves to feel appreciated for her good work, she really feels uncomfortable when they make a big fuss of it. She especially dislikes company parties where she and other top performers are celebrated. A few times she was asked to say a few words to the crowd, and she thought she'd faint. She passionately dislikes speaking in public.

She loves her job and she is nice to everyone without even trying. When a patient rings the bell, she will instantly go to see what she can assist with.

Coming to work, she is always punctual, but she also loves to leave when her time is up. At times, there are too many admissions and/or she has to tend to too many patients during the night, and this will give her a feeling of overwhelm and at times even despair. She

---

[1] - Not her real name

gets really frustrated when she cannot finish in time documenting her rounds and she has to clock out well after her work hours are up.

At home, in dealing with the children, Julia is the "good cop." She often wishes she could be more assertive, but the fact is that when her husband is not at home, the kids do mostly what they want (within certain boundaries, which the children figured out a long time ago). She loves her children very much and she'd do anything for them, but they can wear her out easily after a few hours with them. She feels much more at ease when her husband is around to control them

She is really good at taking time to listen to her kids' and husbands' stories or complaints and often wishes that her kids and husband were at least half as considerate of her feelings as she is to theirs.

Her relationship with her husband is usually great. She allows him to make most of the major decisions and she, in turn, makes most of the household related decisions. If it was up to her, she'd spend most of her time at home with the kids or chatting with friends or family. Luckily, her husband is an outgoing person who takes the family almost weekly out to the ocean, to the nearby park, or even to longer hiking trips.

Considering everything, Julia is happy and content. She loves her family, her job, and life in general.

Julia is a great example of a **high** S style individual.

Communication Style

- ☑ high S style individuals are supportive and caring individuals who place great emphasis on building and maintaining harmonious relationships
- ☑ non-confrontational - because they want to avoid hurting others' feelings, S style individuals do not always express their true feelings; hence, they'll often say whatever will help them avoid conflict and ensure harmony and peace in their relationships.
- ☑ natural great listeners (best of the four styles)

164

- ☑ easy to get along with
- ☑ patient
- ☑ kind and tactful
- ☑ friendly
- ☑ great team-player
- ☑ has great ability to empathize
- ☑ has natural tendency to display a friendly smile during conversation
- ☑ can often come across as shy and/or humble
- ☑ will "shot down" when under stress, feeling disrespected, or when disagreeing with those around them; and might withhold critical information

Strengths and Weaknesses

Here are some of the S style strengths:

- ☑ great listener (the best of the four styles)
- ☑ supportive – derives great satisfaction from helping others
- ☑ non-competitive (unlike D style, and somewhat the I style, individuals who are highly competitive)
- ☑ great followers – they are compliant and easy to manage employees (and great spouses)
- ☑ great at completing what they start
- ☑ consistent, reliable, and dependable
- ☑ cooperative and great team-player
- ☑ patient
- ☑ careful
- ☑ trusting and trustworthy
- ☑ respectful – will try hard not to hurt others' feelings
- ☑ loyal – both in sticking with a workplace and in relationships (again, as their name suggests, they like steadiness and stability in their life)
- ☑ trusting and accepting
- ☑ people pleaser – will go to great extent to ensure that everyone is comfortable and taken care of
- ☑ considerate and treats everyone with respect
- ☑ at work uses methods that have been proven to produce the desired results

- ☑ have great work-ethics
- ☑ do not mind routine work (they often like it)
- ☑ they like to create a "homey," comfortable environment around them
- ☑ they are peace-makers, trying to ensure that everyone around them are heard, respected, and have their needs met; as part of a team, they often act as the "stabilizing factor" trying to keep peace and ensuring that all parties are heard. They will, however, prefer to play the "supportive" role in the team, NOT the "leader" role.
- ☑ Hesitant and cautious – these two behavioral tendencies can be really useful in many instances. For example, when a team of mostly D and I styles are ready to implement a change, launch a new product, or make a major purchase, the S (and C) style's cautious nature will make them ask questions that will clarify potential weak points.
  In teamwork, the S styles hesitant and cautious nature is often a great plus.

It is important to note that each style's "strengths" are truly strengths when used in moderation. As uncle Ben said in the movie *Spiderman* "With great powers come great responsibilities" – and the same applies to each style's strengths. Our strengths are perceived as such only when we keep them under control (or when used responsibly, to use uncle Ben's term). Out of control, regardless of what style one might be, our strengths become weaknesses.

Most of the conflict, misunderstandings, or other types of interpersonal challenges that we get into, are often the result of us pushing our strengths to extremes. Most of us know our weaknesses and we try to stay away from behaviors that make them surface. More often than not, it is our strengths – pushed to extremes - that get us in trouble.

> Your *weaknesses* are often the result of pushing your *strengths* to the extreme.

Here's a list of some of the S style individuals' strengths that turn into weaknesses when pushed to the extreme or get out of control:

Strengths Under Control	Strengths Out of Control
Accepting	Naive
Trusting	
Calm	Passive / No Initiative / Unenthusiastic / Indifferent / Uninvolved / Unemotional
Satisfied	
Careful	Hesitant / Indecisive
Cautious	Holds Back Progress
Conservative	Resistant to Change / Passive Aggressive
Consistent	
Humble	Non-Assertive / "Invisible"
Amiable	Easily Manipulated / Submissive/ Non-Assertive
Considerate	
Cooperative	
Easygoing	
Helpful	
Kind	
Supportive	
Tolerant	
People Pleaser	
Dependable	Predictable
Reliable	
Loyal	... to an extent that at times you allow others to take advantage of you
Good Listener	Non-assertive / Compliant/ Hesitant
Patient	
Sensitive	Easily Hurt / Vulnerable / Timid / Shy / Non-Assertive
Respectful	
Tactful	

Table 6.1 – Steadiness Style: Strengths become weaknesses when pushed to extremes

Challenge Areas

While reading about all the great qualities of the supportive and friendly S style, one wonders if this style could have any shortcomings. But just like any other style, the S style has his/her limitations as well:

- They are calm, friendly, and supportive, but can get frustrated when they need to work side-by-side with fast-paced and bottom-line type people (the outspoken and blunt D)
- Due to their calm and friendly demeanor, they often try to project an unemotional facial expression, even when others obviously hurt their feelings. They tend to NOT express their frustrations; instead they bottle up all their hurts till they can't hold it any longer and then they "blow up", letting it all out in a frustrated, emotional, and angry verbal outburst
- Have difficulty being assertive or take charge (though with practice they can get better at it)
- They tend to be cautious and do not like to be rushed – they need time to digest the information they have available in order to bring good decisions
- As the name of the style suggest, S style individuals love to keep things steady – they do not like sudden change in their careers or at home. Ideally, they want timely heads-up about any upcoming change AND a clear explanation of why the change is necessary. When S style individuals do not understand WHY change is necessary, they might sabotage the process and/or respond with a passive/aggressive attitude.
- The combination of 1) their desire to support others and 2) their attempt to avoid conflict at all cost, they often end up being pushed around or manipulated by others
- They often feel that they have no control over what's going on around them and end up giving in easily to demands and giving up easily. They often easily submit to others' demands and whims
- Can get emotional when under extreme stress or when exposed to stressful news
- Even when stressed, or highly emotional, they do their best to hide their emotions and stress behind a kind smile
- Some S style individuals (especially if an SI combination style) can be a bit sloppy and disorganized

Knowledge is Power! Take control of your weaknesses!

Many of us often perceive the S style individuals around us as the sweetest, kindest people in the world. Some are blessed to have a mother, coworker, or others close by who possess S style traits. It is great to see these people day after day balanced, smiling, and never tired of supporting us and others around them.

While many of us greatly appreciate S style individuals, there are also a great number of people who constantly get frustrated when faced with individuals who display S style behaviors. Even those of us who highly appreciate this style, we at times get frustrated when faced with some of the weaknesses of this style.

If you are an S style individual, understand that most of your strengths – moderate paced, careful, supportive, etc. - are your best allies when dealing with those around you, but at the same time, they are the very traits that at times can make you less effective in maintaining successful relationships.

Remember!

Each of the four sets of behaviors are available to you!

Just like when having access to four bowls of fruits, you might prefer one fruit over the other, but it is up to you to reach in one or the other bowl and consume any of the four fruits.

The same applies to the four styles. They are at your fingertips at all times and it is up to you to reach in any of the four sets of behavior (D, I, S, or C) to make you more effective in any social situation. It might not always feel very comfortable or natural[1], but it is the most effective way to creating and maintaining successful relationships.

Here are some areas where S style individuals can take a conscious effort to bring about some improvement:

---

[1] - **D**'s have difficulty slowing down and listening well; I styles often have difficulty being bottom-line in delivering information; S styles often find it hard to be assertive and direct; and Cs at times find it difficult to loosen up and socialize freely– when we become aware of these blind spots, we can take conscious effort to address them.

- You naturally tend to trust people and are very accepting in nature – all qualities that are highly appreciated by those around you. Watch out, however, not to come across as naïve, nor allow others to take advantage of you

- Learn ways to assert your will whenever you find that others try to take advantage of your kindness and willingness to help. Practice saying – possibly the hardest word for you – the word "NO[1]"

> Your *weaknesses* are often the result of allowing your *strengths* to get out of control.

- Unless you work in an environment where you control the pace of work (counselor, social worker, therapist, yoga instructor[2], etc.), try to realize that your calm and slower pace can come across as having no initiative; or you could even be perceived by some as lazy. An antidote to this is to speed up a bit whenever possible and try to get more involved into tasks that might not seem directly your duty but directly affect your work or workplace.

- You often project an attitude of "no-urgency," which can annoy the D and I styles around you, especially if you are expected to be more involved or work at a faster pace. Try to read your work environment's expectation of you and speed up a bit, if necessary. Again, if you work in an environment where you set the pace – and your pace produces adequate results – and you are happy with your pace, then keep on doing what works for you. (Your attitude of "no-urgency" can also be a strength, since you are able to easily complete tasks that for other styles might seem dull, repetitive, and boring)

- Being cautious and careful might feel very natural to you, but you might often be viewed by others as hesitant and cowardly. Feel free to take some calculated risks – and when the stakes are not too high, even some uncalculated risk - it is ok to make some mistakes. Mistakes are our best teachers (make sure you do not follow my suggestion here if you are a surgeon or pilot –

---

[1] - See Appendix C, on page 252 for more on how to say "No" without feeling that you are offending others

[2] - See page 178 for a list of most popular careers for S style individuals

some jobs just do not lend themselves very well to learn through mistakes ☹)

- You are naturally easygoing, helpful, and dependable, this tells others that they can count on you whenever they need you; and this is really great – we love you for this. Just make sure that no one takes advantage of your willingness to help and end up manipulating you.
- Understand that two of the styles – the D and the C styles – do not place too much emphasis on emotions. On the job, and other business situations, try to steer clear from bringing emotions into your conversations when dealing with these two styles. (Try to stick to the bottom line, facts, and data when dealing with Ds and Cs)
- Each style should take lessons in humility from you, as S styles tend to naturally be really humble individuals. Just remember, it is OK to be more assertive and take credit for your work. You do not want to be seen as shy and unassertive. Practice being assertive (and confident) and you'll notice that the more you do it the easier it gets.
- Taking important decisions <u>quickly </u>is not one of your natural strengths; this can make you look hesitant and indecisive. Replace your hesitancy with assertiveness – just say "Let me chew on it for a minute and I'll get back to you on this in a moment/10 minutes/an hour/by tomorrow" – whatever is appropriate in any particular situation. This will make you look like someone confident and competent; you can then sweat out the agony of bringing a decision in the privacy of your office… or locked in the bathroom. Well, do whatever it takes☺, just make sure you stand by your decision (as long as you know it's a workable "solution").
- On the job, take more initiative to address problem areas, challenges, and other tasks that might not seem urgent to you, but would definitely improve the overall work environment. Do not fall in the S style "trap" of complacency – beat the possible perception of you as being passive and having no initiative!
- Being patient is one of your greatest qualities – especially the D and the I styles would greatly benefit from allowing some of it

to rub on them. Watch out, however, do not be patient to a point to allow others to disrespect you or otherwise overstress you. Speak up and nip in the bud any disrespectful chit-chat! (S style individuals tend to listen patiently – and not say a word – even when someone hurts their feelings or otherwise are disrespectful).

- You naturally dislike change and like to keep your environment, processes, and routines steady around you. However, be careful not to be perceived as an obstacle to progress (in the work environment or at home). If you find yourself in the midst of change, INSTEAD OF sabotaging the process (which is often a natural response of the S individual) try to find out WHY this change is necessary and how will it benefit you and/or your company; and then try to support your teammates in implementing the changes.

- You have a great heart and can be really sensitive at times. However, when you deal with D and C style individuals, they place really little – or no – importance to emotions; as well as I styles, with their constant "blabber" can make comments that can come across to you as insensitive. Just remember that people around you most often do not mean to be insensitive, but simply are differently wired and usually see no harm in their comments. In short, they don't say things to hurt you – they only say things to best express themselves (and we all could take lessons in improving how to most effectively express ourselves, don't we?).

- Commit to spend a few hours regularly with a D style friend or acquaintance and try to model their behavior. Speak up, speed up, show more assertiveness. It is important to spend time with this style so you can model some of their more assertive behaviors. It is doable – it only takes practice.

- If your natural tendency is to be a bit on the sloppy side, learn some organizational skills. Keep documents filed away in clearly labeled folders, keep food and other non-work related items off your desk (and put your zen fountain in the corner of your office on a stand or on the file cabinet vs. on your desk).

Expectations of Others

Here's what S style individuals expect of those around them:

- *Be patient and friendly*
- *Do not shout at me!*
- *Do not push me – let me do things at my own pace*
- *Understand and respect the fact that I'm more in touch with my feelings than the other three styles*
- *Please do not use sarcasm when you talk to me*
- *Listen to what I have to say* (S style individuals are often overly respectful – or even shy – and if not given clear opportunity to speak, they often will not express their needs, wants, concerns, etc.)
- *Do not dump on me sudden changes. If you want to bring about a change, discuss it with me and explain clearly why that change is needed.*
- *Don't abuse my kindness and supportive nature! Just because I don't express it, that does not mean that I don't notice it when you try to take advantage of me...*
  (often coworkers and/or family members will notice the S style individual's tendency to be supportive and helpful, and will – sometimes not even consciously – abuse the S style's willingness and eagerness to help)

How to Deal with Conflict when Dealing with an S Style Individual

S style individuals rarely lose their calm. More often than not, it will be you or someone else who'll bring the conflict about; S style individuals are wired in a way that they'll do anything in their power to avoid conflict. But if you do find yourself in a conflict situation with an S style, here are some tips on how to defuse it.

- Do not raise your voice! S style individuals will "shut down" and will not communicate openly – or will stop communicating completely - if they feel threatened.
- Do not rush them – allow them time to express themselves
- Try to remain calm. S style individuals can easily become defensive and evasive when facing an angry person

- Let them vent – do not interrupt!
- Let them express their feelings
- Once you allowed the S style individual to vent, try to explain your side in a calm manner, with enough detail to clearly show WHY your point is valid (and REMEMBER! rarely is the truth "black" or "white" – more often then not both of you might be right, you just have to come up with a happy medium or a third "option" that will satisfy both of you)
- It they have to bring a decision, provide them adequate time to think (ideally a few hours to a few days)
- Expect to hear comments such as "This makes me feel..." and other feelings related comments. <u>Validate those feelings </u>by saying something like "I understand how that can make you feel upset/sad/etc..." or "I'm sorry to hear that *xyz* upset you – let's see how we can work out a solution..." (try to avoid saying "I understand how you feel" – chances are that you have no idea how they feel)

Most importantly, remember to allow the S style individual to express him, sit back, listen deeply, and keep your calm. Most S style individuals are very compliant and want to do a great job in all areas; and will do whatever possible to keep everyone happy. Of the four styles, they are the easiest to get along with, are most considerate, and are least interested in fighting with you. So take it easy when in conflicting situation with them.

Remember!

In conflict, the truth is rarely "black" or "white" – more often then not both of you might be right; you just have to be willing to take time to understand each other's point of view and...
1. agree to disagree agreeably, or
2. come to the realization that the issue at hand can be viewed in multiple ways and you are both right, or
3. come up with a happy medium (compromise), or
4. synergize: come up with a third option; a solution that will satisfy both of you.

Steadiness Style – the "Real" Best Friend

Do you have a real friend - a best friend? If you do, you are truly blessed, for real friends are not always easy to find. We all have buddies and people who we can have fun with or get along well with; but nothing compares to having a "real" friend – someone that you can trust 100% and can rely on at any time of the day…

Of course any of the styles can be someone's best friend and can have friends and get along just great. But let's pause for a moment and review what does "real friend" mean?

A real friend…

- is trustworthy
- is there for you when you need him or her
- will listen to you <u>patiently</u> when you have something to say, want to share a story, or want to pour out your heart
- will (try to) understand what you're going through
- will help you come up with solutions to your challenges
- accepts you as you are
- is loyal

Do you have such a friend? If you do, chances are that this person is a high S style individual. S style individuals are naturally the best listeners of the four styles, as well as are naturally driven to support those around them.

They are not only best friends in private, but they are also best "buddies" at work. They are the ones who anyone can rely on for help and support or for a shoulder to cry on when one needs to complain about a work-related issue or a burdensome personal issue.

The truth is that anyone of us can reach into our S style behaviors and display great listening skills and be empathetic, but it will never come so naturally to us as it comes to an S style individual.

If you are an I or a D style, do understand that your S style friends will not always have your speed and enthusiasm, but they will be more reliable at completing tasks than most your D or I style coworkers.

And let's not forget one of the other

great traits of S style individuals: loyalty. When you get an S style friend (or employee[1]), they'll stick with you through thick and thin.

S style individuals can be funny, organized, focused, supportive, and reliable – everything that one needs from a real friend or from a good coworker. Appreciate the S style individuals in your environment and let them be your friends – or at least be friendly with them (they deserve it). And occasionally do show your appreciation with small gestures of gratitude, as simple as an invitation for a lunch or simply telling them "Thanks for being such a great friend!"

How to Motivate the S Style Individual

Regardless whether we are talking about an employee, child, a spouse, or significant other, there are a few simple ways to motivate these friendly and supportive individuals. While many of the suggestions below apply mostly to motivating employees, several of the suggestions can be equally applied in other types of relationships as well.

- Smile and <u>be kind</u> with them!
- Provide them with clear, easy to follow instructions on WHAT needs to be done and HOW it needs to be done (they'll most likely follow the process to the letter as you lay it out to them). S style individuals love to follow proven procedures and often do not mind routine work. In fact, they often enjoy the predictability of routine work.
- "I need your help," is one of the key phrases that will make the S type "jump" at a task. S type individuals' supportive tendencies, makes them want to feel useful and they love to support others.
- Praise them for their consistent manner of successfully completing tasks. Express your appreciation for their supportive manner. Simply noticing that their efforts are appreciated, S style individuals will want to do more to support you.
- Provide them plenty of time to complete tasks.
- Do not rush them! When S style individuals feel rushed, they get overly stressed and their performance suffers.
- If you want to implement a change in processes/routine, make sure to let the S style know early on about the upcoming

[1] - An S style employee will stay loyal to their employment place as long as they feel appreciated and respected. Often, even if they dislike their jobs (but feel appreciated and respected) they will not attempt to look for employment elsewhere. They like to keep things steady and stay away from major changes as much as possible.

changes, as well as thoroughly explain WHY those changes are necessary and HOW it will benefit them (and the company). If a high S style individual experiences sudden change (at home or at work) and/or they do not fully understand WHY that change came about – or why was it necessary – they will sabotage the implementation of the change and might adopt a passive aggressive attitude.

- Allow them to work in small teams where their consistent work and supportive nature is appreciated.

Remember!
Motivating others can be "tricky." You can ONLY motivate people to do things they are interested in. Trying to motivate different styles to complete tasks that are totally against their behavioral tendencies can be futile and ineffective. Take the effort to recognize the behavioral style of the person who you are working with and motivate them by allowing them to capitalize on their natural strengths[1].

What Demotivates the S Style Individual

- High-speed environments can be a challenge for the high S style, especially if it involves dealing with lots of change.
- "You are terrible," or similar degrading statements - even if intended as humor - this types of remarks are perceived as very hurtful by S style individuals. Their days are spent in supporting others and they have nothing but good intentions. They really care to be appreciated for their efforts and truly get demotivated when someone gives them negative feedback.
- Working in stressful environments where conflicts – or potential for conflict - arise on a regular basis (either with customers or coworkers)
- An environment where quick decision-taking is necessary. S styles (just like C styles) need time to thoroughly weigh

---

[1] - Have your employee(s) take a DiSC® PPSS (or DiSC 2.0) to ensure that you get an accurate reading of the person's behavioral style. The DiSC profile will also suggest ways to motivate the person most effectively – for more details and to see a sample profile, visit **www.egSebastian.com/assessments**

possibilities before deciding on important (and not so important) issues.

- Working long hours individually, especially if they do not have clear instructions on HOW to complete their tasks properly. (They prefer working in teams; and they need clear directions/instructions/description on how to complete their tasks. When working as part of a team, they always have the option to get the input of teammates; but when working alone, they can get really frustrated if they do not have clear, step-by-step instructions on how to complete their job)
- Being interrupted regularly and multi-tasking can stress the high S individual.
- Working side by side with individuals who tend to be blunt, "overly" fast paced, and/or pushy.
- Working under the supervision of a fast-paced, bottom-line, and blunt manager

S's Most Popular Career Choices[1]

Table 6.2 – S Style Most Popular Career Choices

Animal Care and Service Worker*	Translator and Interpreter *	
Childcare Worker	Athlete	Bus Drivers
Carpenter**	Agricultural Worker	Cashier
Chefs, Cooks, and Food Preparation Worker	Carpet, Floor, and Tile Installers and Finisher**	Correctional Treatment Specialist***
Clergy* + **	Cosmetologist	Counselor
Home Health Aides	Dietitian	Dispatcher
Fashion Designer** or ***	File Clerk**	Flight Attendant
Floral Designer **	Funeral Director	Home Care Aide
Customer Service Representative	Hotel, Motel, and Resort Desk Clerks	Human Service Assistants
Ophthalmic Laboratory Technician**	Licensed Vocational Nurse	Occupational Therapist Assistant and Aide
Registered Nurse	Massage Therapist	Medical Assistant**
Model	Musician	Lodging Manager***
Occupational Therapist	Office Clerk**	Licensed Practical Nurse
Order Clerk	Paralegal** or ***	Personal Aide
Pharmacy Aide**	Photographer	Psychologist
Radiation Therapist	Secretary**	Social Worker
Speech-Language Pathologist	Teacher Assistant	Teller
Veterinarian**	Veterinary Technician	Zookeeper
Nursing Aide	Nutritionist	Interior Designer

---

[1] - in no particular order

* - often in SI combination
** - often in SC combination
*** - often in SCD combination

These are only a few of the careers most S style individuals tend to enjoy due to the many opportunities to work in steady environments with predictable daily routines and/or social settings where they can utilize their strong supportive skills.

If your behavioral style blend contains two (or three) styles at about the same intensity[1] levels, remember to check the most popular career choices for your secondary style as well. If, for example, you are an SC style individual, you'll probably enjoy several of the careers listed in the *C's Most Popular Career Choices* on page 212.

Power Tip #6

Be patient and gentle with the S styles around you!

Most S style individuals around you have nothing but great intentions and an honest desire to support you. They, however, do not always bring decisions and complete tasks at the speed you'd expect them.

Be patient with them - They deserve it!
And when you plan some changes, take time to carefully and kindly explain why certain changes need to be implemented or why certain things need could be done differently, perhaps more effectively...

Of the four styles, the S is the only style who gets great satisfaction from completing tasks in order to help those around them.

Practice patience and kindness when interacting with them and they'll become your greatest helpers and/or friends!

---

[1] To get an accurate idea of what is your behavioral style, complete the valid and reliable DiSC® 2.0, DiSC 2Plus, or DiSC PPSS profile, at **www.egsebastian.com/disc_classic**

Steadiness Style: *Improve Your Relationships and Effectiveness* **Self-Coaching Worksheet**

(Print out a blank self-coaching sheet at **www.egSebastian.com/SelfCoach**)

1. What are my strengths that I'm most proud of?

_____

_____

_____

2. What are some of my strengths that make me most effective in my environment?

_____

_____

_____

3. What are some of my strengths that are (perhaps) perceived as weaknesses in my environment?

_____

_____

_____

4. What are some of my weaknesses that make me less effective in my environment?

_____

_____

_____

5. Based on what I read in this chapter (and on what I already knew), what can I do to become more effective at creating and maintaining successful relationships in my workplace and/or at home? (Pages 168 - 171)

_____

_____

_____

6. Based on what I read in this chapter (and on what I already knew), what can I do to become more effective at setting and accomplishing personal and professional goals? (Pages 168 -171)

_____

_____

_____

_____

_____

_____

_____

7. Is it an option to speak to my supervisor (or coworkers) and ask to be assigned tasks that are more in line with my strengths? If yes, how would I approach him/her/them about it?

_____

_____

_____

_____

8. What else can I do to become more effective in all areas of my life? (Based on what you read – e.g., talk to spouse or significant other about your style and your style's needs, behavioral tendencies; how can you improve your relationship with loved ones, etc.)

_____

_____

_____

_____

_____

_____

_____

Important!

The DISC Behavioral System was **NOT** designed to label or to judge the individuals around us. It is simply a tool that can help better understand your own behavior and the behavioral tendencies and needs of the people you interact with on a daily basis.

This understanding of behavioral tendencies and the needs of each style can help improve your communication and relationships with everyone around you.

Chapter 7

The Conscientiousness Style

- The Conscientiousness (C) Style – Quick Overview
- How to Easily Recognize a C Style Individual
- Systematic Tom
- Communication Style
- Strengths and Weaknesses
- Challenge Areas
- Knowledge is Power! Take control of your weaknesses!
- Expectations of Others
- How to Deal with Conflict when Dealing with a C Style Individual
- Conscientiousness Style – The Critical Thinker
- How to Motivate the C Style Individual
- What Demotivates the C Style Individual
- C Style Most Popular Career Choices
- Power Tip #6: Develop a Deep Appreciation for the C Styles in Your Environment
- Conscientiousness Style: Self-Coaching Worksheet

Famous High C Examples:

- Bill Gates
- Martha Stuart
- Sandra Bullock
- Jenifer Aniston, in the movie *The Break-Up*
- Steve Martin, in the movie *Shopgirl*
- Robin Williams, in the movie *Final Cut*

The Conscientiousness (C) Style – Quick Overview

> ***Conscientiousness (C) - moderate paced** and **task oriented***
> C's are careful and detail oriented people who love to work with
> tasks and concepts; they like to plan their work and are committed to
> quality and accuracy in all areas.

- ☑ Do you tend to move and talk at a more moderate pace?
- ☑ Do you prefer working with numbers, concepts, and other task oriented activities (vs. working with people)?
- ☑ Do you tend to be cautious – or at times hesitant - when faced with unknown situations (on the job or in your personal life)?
- ☑ Do you tend to have high expectations of everyone around you?
- ☑ Do you dislike sudden changes that affect your routine at work or at home?
- ☑ Do you like to plan your work and follow the plan closely?
- ☑ Do you tend to be organized, analytical, and detail-oriented?
- ☑ Do you tend to take your time to make good decisions?
- ☑ Do you believe that rules and procedures were made to be followed?
- ☑ Do you take pride in your work and strive for perfection (or close to perfection)?

If you answered "yes" to most of these questions, then you most likely are a high C –Conscientiousness - style[1] individual, or a combination of two or more styles with some high C style traits.

Or perhaps you know someone in your environment who fits this description. If yes, it is most likely that this person is a C style individual and displays most of the behaviors described in this chapter.

---

[1] To get an accurate idea of what is your behavioral style, complete the valid and reliable DiSC® 2.0, DiSC 2Plus, or DiSC PPSS profile, at **www.egsebastian.com/disc_classic**

Figure 7.1 – C style individuals often come across as cautious and detail oriented

Whenever we need help with some complex tasks that need great attention to detail and/or accuracy - such as tax preparation, complex calculations, in-depth analysis of something; or even help with technical issues, such as building or fixing a computer, or learning to use a software or computer program - we instinctively enlist the help of the C style individuals in our environment.

C style individuals have excellent technical skills, ability to pay attention to detail, and have great abilities at getting and staying organized.

We all highly admire C style individuals' superior ability to stay focused, great technical skills, and ability to stay organized; however – just like any other style - the very strength they possess can turn into weaknesses that can be perceived as extremely frustrating by those around them. For example, when they are nit-picking on every little detail or "flaw" they perceive and step into their "perfectionist" mode; when they are way too hesitant to move on – or move to action - because of lack of every detail they think they need; or when they refuse to laugh at our jokes or show appreciation for our humorous stories (in the workplace most C's are 100% focused on the job at hand and do not like to be sidetracked with chit-chat or "meaningless" socializing).

When in the right environment, the C style's strengths are priceless. They are our pilots, surgeons, engineers, software developers, and other[1] great minds who fill jobs that require tenacity, focus, and excellent attention to detail.

Individuals who are more moderate paced (both in physical movement and speech) and are more interested in working with tasks and concepts, tend to adopt mostly behaviors from the Conscientiousness set of behaviors (pg. 188) and we call them Conscientiousness (C) Style individuals. This chapter is dedicated to describing in detail the behavioral tendencies of Conscientiousness (C) style individuals.

When a person tends to adopt mostly behaviors from the Conscientiousness (C) Style set of behaveviors on a consistent basis, this person would be called a
C Style individual
(or Conscientiousness Style Individual)

C style individuals have a tendency to analyze - and often overanalyze - mostly anything that interests or affects them (or perceive that affects them) and have a desire to attain accuracy in whatever they deal with. These tendencies often result in C style individuals being very cautious, thorough, and particular about most things they do.

When communicating with others they often come across as distant, formal, and non-emotional[2]. In their conversations they often engage into in-depth descriptions of technical or task-related topics. When it comes to technical data or other areas of their expertise, C style individuals can be super-verbose, often leaving the listener lost in a torrent of technical terms, data, and in-depth description of the topic...

Approximate percentage of high S style individuals in the US:

Men - 27%

Women 27%

---

[1] - For a more detailed list of careers C style individuals tend to choose and enjoy, see page 212 - 214

[2] "non-emotional" in the sense of NOT allowing themselves to be distracted by others' humor, stories, or small talk; they give 100% attention to the tasks they work on

– Moderate Paced/Task Oriented –
The Conscientiousness (C) Behavioral Style

Conscientiousness style individuals tend to consistently adopt **most** of the following behaviors:

General Tendencies:
- ☑ Tends to talk and move at a more moderate pace
- ☑ Has high expectations of those around him
- ☑ Tends to stay away from risky behaviors and risky unsafe environments
- ☑ Likes to plan his work and activities, and likes to stick to the plan as closely as possible
- ☑ Takes pride in her work and is really good at what she does
- ☑ On the job, she likes to know exactly what her duties are
- ☑ Does not mind routine and repetitive tasks
- ☑ Usually finishes what she starts
- ☑ Gets energized when working on her own on, on tasks, numbers, or concepts (vs. working with people)
- ☑ Is highly dependable, analytical, methodical, and detail-oriented person
- ☑ Believes that rules were made to be followed

Communication Style
- ☑ Talks at a moderate pace and focuses on the bottom line
- ☑ At work tries to avoid small talk and give 100% focus to the task(s) at hand
- ☑ Displays great self-control; often can come across as someone who weighs every word before speaking
- ☑ Doesn't like to be rushed
- ☑ Is cautious – especially with people she doesn't know well - and can come across as hesitant and/or suspicious
- ☑ Tends to be introverted; tries to keep conversations on job-related or other non-personal topics

Conscientiousness Style Motto:
- ☑ "Measure twice, cut once!"

Of the four styles, the C style individuals are the hardest to get to know at a personal level. They tend to be very private and do not open up easily. I believe a great comparison would be to compare them to an onion (or a cabbage, if you don't like onions). It takes time and work to peel off each layer. But if you do take the time to get to know them, you'll often find that they are some amazing people with some great strengths.

While they work they do not like to engage in small talk and often respond to others' attempts to chit-chat with a cold "poker" face clearly communicating with their body language that they are there to work not to socialize.

At work or at home, most C style individuals seem to be humor-handicapped; however, there are many C style individuals – mostly CS and CI behavioral combination individuals – who have excellent sense of humor and display better social skills than the pure C or the CD combination individuals.

When it comes to career choice, C style individuals tend to choose jobs that are technical in nature, perhaps involves research, working with numbers, or involves other task-oriented activities. When in such environment they are very reliable and conscientious workers; they have great follow-through and tend to consistently produce high quality results. They, however, do not always feel comfortable in social settings, such as company parties or, at times, even have difficulty conducting small talk with coworkers or customers.

Unlike the D and I styles who are great at starting new tasks, C style individuals will analyze first all angles, including WHY they'd even consider getting involved with a specific task, and will only proceed when they understand WHY this task should be done and gain a clear understanding on HOW this task could be completed. However, unlike the D and I styles who are poor finishers, when the C style gets started with a project they'll stick with it till completion.

Of the four styles, C style individuals are the most reliable, knowledgeable, and professional individuals we'll ever meet. When, however, they abuse their strengths, they will come across as nitpicky, perfectionist, and antisocial.

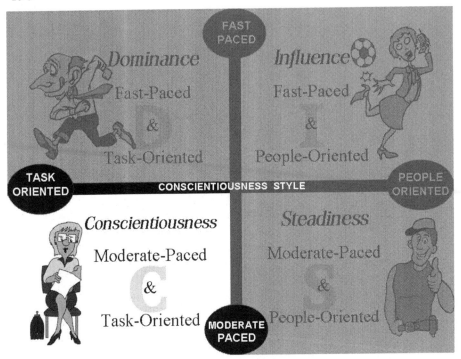

Figure 7.2 – The Conscientiousness Style: Moderate Paced & Task Oriented

How to Easily Recognize a C Style Individual

While most of us are a combination of two or more styles, most of us have a dominant style which is rather easy to spot.

C style individuals can be recognized by noticing their more moderate pace - both in their rate of speech and physical movement - combined with a genuine interest in technical and/or conceptual tasks and data (Fig. 7.2). They tend to consistently come across as detail oriented, cautious, analytical, organized, systematic, and strict followers of rules and procedures.

They have the ability to focus for long periods of time on whatever they are working on, usually are highly organized and systematic, strive for excellence in whatever they do, and like to work at a steady pace without being rushed.

When visiting them in their office or their home environment, one will notice perfect order – everything having their exact place. Try to move something and they'll put it right back to "where it belongs." In the office it will not be uncommon to have blank walls – no pictures or posters, except perhaps posters of rules and regulations – and their desk is perfectly clean, only with the file(s) that they are working on and one or two pieces of stationery.

Systematic Tom

Tom owns a computer retail and repair shop. He works every day from 6:00 am till 4:00 pm., with one hour drive each way. He gets home at about 5:00 pm and he goes through the same routine every day. He enters the house, changes into his "gardening" cloth and he gets in the back (or front) yard to do some raking, weeding, fertilizing, or whatever is needed. He then goes back in, takes a shower, eats, and takes a short (15 to 20 minutes) nap. He'll spend the rest of the day, watching TV (mostly surfing the news channels), or occasionally talking to friends on Skype (internet audio-video chat program).

Tom really enjoys his job. He enjoys the predictability of what could go wrong on a computer that they bring in for repair, he enjoys trouble shooting and finding the problems, and especially loves taking them apart and fixing the electronic equipment. He at times feels like a surgeon – he derives great pleasure out of "bringing back to life" damaged electronic equipment.

Tom's income varies from $2000 to $5000 a month. There are good months and there are some bad months. In the good months he often has to say "No" to lots of work, and he almost always says "No" to urgent work (work that would need to be done the same day or by next day). He does not like to be rushed; he believes that he has a very important job and feels he needs enough time to provide the quality his customers expect from him. In the past, he did refuse to do jobs for several larger companies, due to the high volume that they'd bring in regularly or because they needed the work done on the same day or by next day. Many of these clients never came back.

He also regularly loses clients because he is not opened after 4:00 pm; therefore those who work during the day have no access to him.

Many of Tom's friends and family members suggested that he should hire at least one more employee or keep longer hours at least once or twice a week. If he hired another employee, that employee could work from noon till 7:00 pm (at least twice a week). However, Tom does not want to have the hassle to deal with payroll and other hiring-procedure related paperwork; besides he is afraid to "rock the boat" when things go well as they are.

Tom's family and friends enjoy the aesthetic, organized environment that Tom created at home , and they also look up to Tom for his success in his small business. They also enjoy the ability to ask Tom for advice on computer and computer software related issues; though they often get much more than what they bargained for, as Tom goes into loooooong in-depth technical details about the issue and beyond the issue that they bring up.

When discussing non-technical related topics with Tom, he is usually a great listener, but often is very critical of whatever is being discussed. He likes to stay on the safe side of things and often expresses dislike of uncalculated risks. His friends and family members also got to accept the fact that Tom does not always get the humor that they share around him and he often can be rather dry and bottom-line in his conversations.

All things considered, Tom is liked and is highly valued by most people around him for his reliability, systematic approach to planning and working his plan, display of maturity, diplomacy, great organization skills, and his excellent technical and analytical skills.

Tom is a great example of a high C style individual.

Communication Style

- ☑ High C style individuals are highly task-oriented in their communication, often going into great technical – or otherwise in-depth – details on the topic of discussion.

- ☑ Usually are very diplomatic and polite (at times too polite and too conventional).

- ☑ Of the four styles, C style individuals tend to be most introverted, sharing only the minimum information they feel is necessary

- ☑ They speak at a more moderate pace, often creating the impression that they thoroughly weigh every word they say (of the four styles, the C style is the one who is most self-conscious about what they say, and the DO weigh carefully most of what they say).

- ☑ Usually are withdrawn and talk only in short sentences, focusing only on the bottom line; the exception being when the topic of discussion is within their area of expertise or passion, in which case they'll get to share more details than most people can possibly comprehend.

- ☑ Due to their extreme focus on the tasks that they are working on and their commitment to bringing about excellent results, they will often refuse to engage in small-talk and can come across as cold, unemotional, and even anti-social. Fact is, however, that their "wiring" is such that their priority is to produce excellent results; therefore for them "normal" behavior translates into taking care of business first and "then we can chat."

- ☑ They like to thoroughly understand whatever they are involved in and will ask a plethora of questions in order to acquire the data they need to get a clear picture.

- ☑ They are very analytical in nature, which makes them very effective in performing their tasks; however, it can become a social-interaction hindrance when questioning others' statements or treating them with suspicion (which does happen regularly).

- ☑ They tend to display little to no emotions and have very controlled body language.

☑ They have great respect for data and verifiable facts, and always appreciate it when others come to them prepared to support their claims, suggestions, etc. with data and facts.

☑ They do not like to be pressured into taking quick decisions – they need time to gather the necessary information and data, and analyze the situation thoroughly in order to bring their decisions.

☑ Can come across as someone who lacks passion and is not interested in what's going on around them; however, anyone who's been around a high C knows better. They are very observant and are very interested in whatever affects their environment, their work, and their routines; except they tend to keep their emotions in check and can come across as uninterested in what's going on.

☑ Often very knowledgeable and a great resource of solutions to technical and analytical problems; HOWEVER, they'll rarely volunteer their knowledge. They'll usually share their ideas only if asked for their input

☑ If you got on their "black list," they might withhold data from you or might refuse to help you (which they'll usually decline in a very diplomatic manner).

☑ When conflicting situations arise, they tend to use an indirect approach to resolving it, often trying to resolve the situation through diplomacy and often avoid discussing the real issues.

☑ Will develop friendships and good working relationships based on common interests, not based on emotions (unlike the S and I styles who will often form friendships simply based on whether they have a good feeling about someone or not).

Strengths and Weaknesses

Here are some of the C style strengths:

☑ great ability to pay attention to details
☑ high commitment to creating accurate and excellent work
☑ great ability to organize, plan, and execute

- ☑ thinks through every possibility before bringing a decision (analytical)
- ☑ very careful at completing tasks, often striving for perfection
- ☑ great at completing what they start
- ☑ consistent, reliable, and dependable
- ☑ patient (when working on tasks; not too patient when dealing with people)
- ☑ trustworthy
- ☑ diplomatic
- ☑ modest
- ☑ loyal to their workplace (when allowed to capitalize on their strengths)
- ☑ have great work-ethics
- ☑ do not mind routine work (they often like it)
- ☑ respect and follow rules
- ☑ tend to be conservative in nature
- ☑ great ability to focus for extended periods on tasks
- ☑ great at developing and implementing systematic approaches to completing tasks or to solving problems

It is important to note that each style's "strengths" are truly strengths when used in moderation. As uncle Ben said in the movie *Spiderman* "With great powers come great responsibilities" – and the same applies to each style's strengths. Our strengths are perceived as such only when we keep them under control (or when used responsibly, to use uncle Ben's term). Out of control, regardless of what style one might be, our strengths become weaknesses.

> Your *weaknesses* are often the result of pushing your *strengths* to the extreme.

Here's a list of some of the C style strengths that turn into weaknesses when pushed to the extreme or get out of control:

Strengths Under Control	Strengths Out of Control
Accurate	Nitpicky / Slow / Hesitant Obsessive / Stubborn / Worrisome / Hard-to-Please / Unpopular
Careful	
Conscientious	
Detail Oriented	
Systematic	
Thorough	
Conservative	Holds back progress / Fun-Buster
Analytical	Nitpicky / Slow / Cold / Distant / Suspicious / Distrustful / Critical / Unfriendly / Unforgiving / Hesitant
Consistent	Predictable / Boring / Unwilling to take on new duties
Focused	
Formal	Distant / Unfriendly / Withdrawn / Unpopular / Insecure
Diplomatic	
Good Self-Control	Cold / Distant / Uninterested / Uninvolved / Unfriendly / Introverted / Unemotional / Uncommunicative / Unpopular
Loyal	Dependent
Modest	Invisible / Shy
Organized	Nitpicky / Worrisome / Obsessive / Perfectionist / Resentful / Critical / Overly Sensitive
Perfectionist	Revengeful / Over-Sensitive / Alienating / Pessimistic / Hard-to-Please / Unforgiving
Respectful	Shy / Withdrawn / Unaffectionate
Schedules & Plans	Rigid / Predictable / Resentful / Inconsiderate

Table 7.1 – Conscientiousness Style: Strengths become weaknesses when pushed to extremes

Challenge Areas

Like any of the other styles, the organized and conscientious C style individuals too have their dose of challenge areas:

- In an attempt to create perfection, follow rules, and take care of all details, the C style individual often lives in a constant state of worry. Much of the worry is about fear of NOT meeting their own standards; but they also constantly worry about making sure they have everything in its place, be punctual, be accurate, etc.
- Careful and detail oriented when it comes to tasks, but not so careful and attentive when it comes to relationships; C style individuals worry about - and give too much importance - to the things around them and their relationships are often of secondary importance
- Displaying emotions and feelings does not always come naturally to high C style individuals, nor do they feel that it's a priority, especially on the job and other professional environments; hence it affects them little to none when they see others display their emotions – this tendency makes them at times come across as indifferent, inconsiderate, and distant
- They will avoid conflicting situations by giving in to the other person and tend NOT to express their frustrations, but rather bottle their hurts up and get back to the other person in "creative" ways (revengeful), often in the form of withholding information or refusing support
- Tends to be overly analytical and questioning, which often translates into treating those around them with suspicion; which, in turn, results in difficult relationships
- At times has difficulty being assertive or take charge (though with practice they can get better at it)
- Loves to follow own routine and plan, which can often be viewed by others as rigid, robotic, and unreasonable
- Tests everyone's patience, and often annoys those around them (except other high C styles), with their constant tendency to overanalyze and over-think things

- At times can get too obsessed or stuck on overanalyzing the smallest details, which often results in hesitation to move ahead with tasks and/or slows down processes considerably
- Just like the S style, C style individuals too have difficulty coping with sudden changes in their environment; helping them understand WHY those changes are needed and WHY they are needed will considerably speed up their acceptance and support of the coming changes
- Tends to be too formal and is unable to relax and freely enjoy others' company
- Has unrealistically high expectations of those around them, which often results in others feeling uneasy for not being able to meet their high standards, and/or will perceive the C style as perfectionist and nitpicky(just like any other style, they believe their behaviors are the "normal" ones and everyone should be organized, careful, and detail-oriented just like them)
- During social events – or at times even at work - can come across as shy or even antisocial due to their tendency to be withdrawn and their natural tendency towards acting more as an observer than an actual participant
- Can become defensive when they – or their work - are criticized (they've spent endless hours on considering every angle and possibility and believe they chose the best possible solution; so it is really upsetting for them when someone can, in the spur of the moment, criticize their work)
- They expect more from themselves than anyone else expects from them
- Loyalty is a great strength of the C style; however, at times this can translate into dependency, sticking around with a job (or a relationship) where they do not feel appreciated or are not satisfied with (often resistance to change and the tendency to want to preserve the status-quo are the main hold-back factors to moving on)
- At times they are overly critical with those around them and are often unable to maintain healthy relationships due to their

> Your *weaknesses* are often the result of allowing your *strengths* to be pushed to the extreme.

constant tendency to judge others for their "sloppiness," "disorganization," and other "nonconformist" tendencies

- Will spend hours or days frustrated, worried, or stressed (at times even mildly depressed) due to not meeting their own perfectionist standards

Knowledge is Power! Take control of your weaknesses!

Ah..., it'd be so nice if we could all be as organized, disciplined, and conscientious as our C style friends. We'd all have well-organized offices and homes, we'd always know where to find anything we need, we'd plan our days and meals, and we'd live happily ever after as laid out by our own plan. But before we get too melancholic and envious about all the great qualities C style individuals possess, we have to face it that they too have their limitations.

If you are a C style individual, it is often clear to you that life would be much easier if everyone could just get their act together and live more planned and organized lives; and you are probably right, we all would definitely benefit greatly if we'd learn to be more organized. However, your great analytical, organizational, and other great task-oriented skills come with their own baggage of areas that could take some improvement.

Here are some of the areas that you could improve upon that would make your life and the lives of those around you a bit easier:

- Everything has its place and that's great; but try to relax a bit and not be too obsessed with order. While your natural wiring is to stay on top of things by keeping everything where they belong, to others you might come across as nitpicky and obsessive. When you are in the company of friends or coworkers, try to focus more on nurturing your relationships and less on "who touches what" and "who puts things down the wrong way or in the wrong place." You can always put things back in their place later. Of course, on the job – especially if you are a manager – it does help if you "train" those around you to keep things where they belong; after all, in the long run it does affect the bottom line. But again, make sure that you do not stress about it, but rather enjoy your relationships and take care of "what belongs where" after you nurtured your relationships first.

- Smile!

Though we all met C styl individuals who display a "natural abilitiy" to smile, many C style individuals (just like D styles) tend to keep a somber, almost angry facial expression; and then they wonder why people are afraid of them, avoid them, or do not socialize much with them.

Smile...

- when someone is talking to you (do not grin – simply show interest in what you are hearing and do it with a slight smile)
- when you are asking for a favor
- when you conduct small talk
- when you provide customer service
- when you talk to (your) children... and when you listen to their stories
- when you remind someone about procedures or other job-related tasks

I'm not suggesting that you be a smiling machine, but if you are a high C, you know that smiling is not your strengths AND it is one of the biggest reason why you have fewer successful relationships than you'd like to have. When you do smile, you tell those around you that "it's ok to talk to me – I'm approachable." Especially the S and the I styles, they need your smile - that's just how they are built. The D and C style individuals around you can probably handle the smile-free-you, but just for practice sake, do smile regularly with everyone.

- Be more accepting with those around you! Your natural tendency is to analyze, criticize, and judge the actions of those around you. Try to understand that people around you are not weird – they are simply differently wired and they are perfectly normal as they are. Try to recognize the style of everyone around you and appreciate their strengths; and understand and accept that each style has its weaknesses (including your style) – that's just how we were built. Instead of analyzing and criticizing those around you and getting annoyed by others' shortcomings, simply embrace everyone's differences and focus on maintaining good relationships with everyone around you.

> Try to understand that people around you are not weird – they are simply differently wired and they are perfectly normal as they are. Try to recognize the style of everyone around you and appreciate their strengths; and understand and accept that each style has its weaknesses – that's just how we were built.

- Unless you work in an environment where you control the pace of work (accountant, attorney, engineer, researcher[1], etc.), try to realize that your analytical nature, great attention to detail, and slower pace can come across as being slow and having no initiative; or you could even be perceived by some as lazy. Whenever possible try to speed up a bit, especially where high quality or attention to detail is not a top requirement.

- Just like the S style, you too at times can project an attitude of "no-urgency," which can annoy the D and I styles around you, especially if you are expected to be more involved or work at a faster pace. Try to "read" your work environment's expectation of you and speed up a bit, if necessary. Again, if you work in an environment where you set the pace – and your pace produces adequate results – and you are happy with your pace, then keep on doing what works for you. (Your attitude of "no-urgency" can also be a strength, since you are able to easily complete tasks that for other styles might seem dull, repetitive, and/or requires great attention to details)

- Understand that two of the styles – the S and the I styles –are very much in touch with their emotions. Regardless where these two styles are, they will either express their emotions freely (I style) or can be highly emotional and easily offended (S style). Your primary focus is accomplishing accurate results; but when in teamwork, you will become more effective at accomplishing your goals if you respect and are more considerate of the feelings of those around you. An occasional smile, a listening ear, and communicating with a little more warmth whenever possible will show the I and S styles around you that you are not a stone-cold "robot"

- Taking important decisions <u>quickly</u> is not one of your natural strengths; and while your natural tendency is to analyze all angles before you can proceed, you can be viewed by D and I styles as hesitant and indecisive. Replace your hesitancy with assertiveness – just say "Give me a minute and I'll get back to you on this by 3:00 PM/in 10 minutes/within an hour/by tomorrow/etc." – whatever is appropriate and acceptable in any particular situation. This will make you look like someone confident and competent; you can then analyze the situation or the data in the privacy of your office and come back with a well-thought-out   decision.
  Do understand that those around you respect your deep thinking, but they do want to see you assertive and in charge (especially if

---

[1] - See page 212 – 214 for a detailed list of most popular careers for C style individuals

you are in a leadership position). Of course, if you are surrounded mostly by C and S style individuals, you can take all your time to bring a decision, since you are among people who'd do the exact same thing in your place.

- Just like your S style "neighbor," you naturally dislike change and like to keep your environment, processes, and routines steady around you. However, be careful not to be perceived as an obstacle to progress (in the work environment or at home). If you find yourself in the midst of change, instead of sabotaging the process (which at times can be a natural response of C style individuals) try to find out WHY this change is necessary and HOW will it benefit you and/or your company; and use your conceptual and analytical skills to support your teammates in implementing the changes.

- *Loyalty* is one of your great strengths; but do realize that it can backfire at times when you are loyal to the wrong employer (or the wrong person). Understand that sometimes change is much less painful than staying in a rotten relationship, such as a job that is completely dissatisfying or a job where your excellent strengths are not appreciated. Before you take a dramatic step and part from your current employer (or other type of relationship), be sure to discuss the issues that bother you; often that's all it takes to improve upon your current situation.

- You are a person who naturally loves to follow processes and routines. Periodically re-evaluate your habitual ways to ensure that you are not "loyal" to some outdated or less effective processes or routines.

- Your natural tendency is to be unforgiving and you often hold grudges against others for long periods of time. Now armed with the knowledge assimilated from this book, you probably have a deeper understanding why some people around you are so "strange": emotional and "soft" (S style); goofy, indiscrete, and disorganized (I style); or always in a rush, pushy, and blunt in their communication (D style). We are all designed by nature in a way that we UNINTENTIONALLY step on each others' toes. Different styles often view differences as bad or undesirable and these differences can often translate into severed relationships. However, now that you understand the different styles, you will have a better understanding why those around you behave the way they do and it will be up to you NOT to take "strange" behaviors personally but rather understand that everyone behaves just as their internal "computer program" – one's natural behavioral style - directs them to behave. We are simply different, and "different" is not good or bad – it is simply what it is: different. Forgiveness is an art – one that can be easily mastered through practice; and it starts with raising your acceptance of those around you by better understanding WHY everyone behaves the way they do. So let go of your grudges – forgive those who "sinned" against you – and start treating those who are different from you with understanding and the diplomacy that comes so naturally to you.

- When a "sticky" or conflicting situation arises, instead of walking away from it (and holding a grudge), politely bring it up to the other person and discuss it. Often, simply mentioning the issue that bothers you will take care of itself. At other times you'll have to discuss it and could even end up in a bit of a conflict. However, do understand that some conflict is healthy at times, because it will bring closure and a solution to the issue that was bothering you.
Caution! Some conflicting situations are only YOUR perception. Occasionally your unrealistically high expectations regarding procedures, order, manners, etc. will at times not be met. In these situations there isn't really a conflict to solve, but you simply need to attempt to accept the situation. If, for example, you know that you like your stapler in a certain position on the left side of your desk, but people keep putting it on the wrong side of your desk after they borrow it, simply just put the stapler where you like it to be. After all, it only takes 1 second (and if you do fuss about it regularly, you'll be viewed as nitpicky and a weirdo). Or, if some of your coworkers are regularly humorous and laugh loudly around you – something that might bother you – just let them be. We are all different – their wiring is to socialize more and they have a high need for humor and laughter in their daily "routines."
Bottom line: Do not shy away from conflict, but do choose your "battles" wisely. Do not try to change the people around you; but do not allow anyone to disrespect you or take advantage of you either.

- Spend a few hours regularly with a sky high I style individual. Allow yourself to be sucked into her "funny" world and try to play along. For you to develop better social skills – and be viewed as more fun by your family members and coworkers (if that's a goal of yours) – your best training is to hang out regularly with a sky high I and try to relax and do what she does: laugh at silly things, tell a few personal stories, fake some enthusiasm about something (or maybe you don't have to fake it, maybe you were just holding back). Try to understand the world of a sky high I individual; with this you'll get to better understand your "nemesis" while you'll also learn to relax a bit and learn to be more sociable.

- Try to worry less. Life is not only short but it also a one-time deal – do not spend it worrying most of the time. Your natural wiring will take care of you doing a great job at whatever you touch, and an occasional mistake is only human. No one around you expects you to be perfect –that's only your unrealistic expectation of yourself. Relax! Learn some mediation and relaxation exercises and do them regularly. Socialize and let go of your high expectations. Enjoy life and learn to appreciate and enjoy the people around you. "Things" can be important at times, but it is our social ties that make life great or miserable ☺

Remember!

Each of the four sets of behaviors are available to you!

Just like when having access to four bowls of fruits, you might prefer one fruit over the other, but it is up to you to reach in one or the other bowl and consume any of the four fruits.

The same applies to the four styles. They are at your fingertips at all times and it is up to you to reach in any of the four sets of behavior (D, I, S, or C) to make you more effective in any social situation. It might not always feel very comfortable or natural[1], but it is the most effective way to creating and maintaining successful relationships.

---

[1] - **D**'s have difficulty slowing down and listening well; I styles often have difficulty being bottom-line in delivering information; S styles often find it hard to be assertive and direct; and **C**s at times find it difficult to loosen up and socialize freely– when we become aware of these blind spots, we can take conscious effort to address them.

Expectations of Others

Here's what C style individuals expect of you:

- *When you talk to me, stick to facts and data*
- *Be brief and to the point*
- *Be prepared! Know what you are talking about*
- *At work, avoid stories, jokes, and other non-work related chit-chat*
- *Please don't waist my time with expressing feelings, sentiments, and emotions - Let's just stick to the bottom line!*
- *Don't rush me – let me do things at my own pace*
- *Let me finish what I start – do not interrupt me nor distract me. I like working on tasks on my own and I'd appreciate it if you did NOT try to entertain me or engage in small talk while I work*
- *Show appreciation of my strengths*
- *Understand and respect the fact that details, accuracy, and order are of primary importance to me*
- *If you work close to me, please do not be messy, loud, late, or sloppy*
- *Please try to avoid sarcasm when you talk to me*
  (I styles, and somewhat D's, can deal with sarcastic remarks; but C and S styles, ca get really offended by such remarks and will often carry that hurt for a looong time)
- *Listen to what I have to say and please do not interrupt me*
  (C style individuals are often too diplomatic, cautious, or withdrawn – or even shy – and if not given clear opportunity or encouragement to speak, they often will NOT express themselves fully. If interrupted, they'll often not push to finish what they started saying, even though they might have the correct solution to the issue in discussion.)
- *Do not dump on me sudden changes. If you want to bring about a change, discuss it with me and explain clearly WHY that change is needed.*

How to Deal with Conflict when Dealing with a C Style Individual

C style individuals are usually rather controlled and calm. And while they will tend to resolve most conflicting situations in a diplomatic way, one can usually read quite easily from their body language and facial expression that they are upset. If you do find yourself in a conflict situation with a C style individual, here are some tips on how to defuse it.

- Understand that once they notice "injustices[1]," got offended from something someone said or did, or feel that they were treated unjustly, they'll often react by "shutting down" and refusing to talk, or will just talk the minimum polite talk. Sometimes you'll have to wait for days (or only hours if you are lucky) till they'll be willing to talk about the issue. Half of the time you won't even know that you have a conflicting situation with a C style individual, until they processed it properly and talk it out. At times, however, they'll just internalize it and hold a grudge forever. And "forever" is really only a slight exaggeration; once you offend a C style individual, it will take some hard work to redeem yourself. You can start by consistently speaking their "language," as described in their *Expectations of Others*, on Page 205 and (re)gain their respect by showing that you are considerate to their needs and by expressing appreciation of their strengths.
- Do not raise your voice! C style individuals tend to be very formal and diplomatic and expect the same from others. However, when pressured or cornered they can easily switch into "verbal attack" mode.
- Allow enough time to express themselves
- Avoid being blunt or otherwise too straightforward. While D and I style individuals will appreciate if you say things out openly, and even bluntly, C style individuals prefer to get "sticky" information in a more diplomatic and sensitive format.

---

[1] - "injustices" = someone moved one or more of the objects out of "their place"; their job duties or description was changed without warning and explanation; someone performed a task that was the C style's job; someone didn't do what he was supposed to do; etc.

- Do not rush them, do not interrupt, and maintain your calm. C style individuals can easily become evasive or even defensive when they feel like they do not get the attention they deserve.
- Let them vent – do not interrupt!
- Even if their reasoning sounds unreasonable, validate: say "I'm sorry to hear that xy made you feel that way. Let's try to come up with a solution that will be a win-win for both of us."
- Once you allowed the C style individual to vent, explain your side in a calm manner, with enough solid facts and data to clearly show WHY your point is valid
- Try to keep any reference to emotions or feelings out of the conversation. C style individuals are naturally more fact and solid data oriented people and they'll be more receptive to one's argument when communicating with them using numbers, data, statistics, and other hard facts.
- Whenever possible, quote rules and regulations to support your points
- It they have to bring a decision, provide them adequate time to think it through (ideally a few hours to a few days)
- Understand that most of the time your C style "opponent" knows undoubtedly that she is right – she has thoroughly thought through and perhaps even researched the topic that you are in conflict about... or perhaps you are in conflict about a habit or process that the C style has been using... Either way, you better be ready to back up and prove your statements with solid data and facts, in a calm manner. The only way to change a C style individual's conviction about something is if you can prove your point through hard facts.

Remember!

In conflict, the truth is rarely "black" or "white" – more often then not both of you might be right; you just have to be willing to take time to understand each other's point of view and...

1. agree to disagree agreeably, or
2. come to the realization that the issue at hand can be viewed in multiple ways and you are both right, or
3. come up with a happy medium (compromise), or
4. synergize: come up with a third option; a solution that will satisfy both of you.

Conscientiousness Style – the Critical Thinker

Of the four styles, the C style individuals around you are the ones who have the ability to think most objectively. The inpatient D style individuals rarely take the time to think at the deep levels that C's are able to; and I and S style individuals are often unable to think totally clearly due to mixing emotions into their thinking processes. This is not to say that the D, I, and S style individuals can't think deeply – they certainly can, if they choose to. However, it does not come to them as naturally as for C style individuals.

We all can choose to sit down and really think through something, such as carefully preparing a report, preparing our taxes, or some other task that requires absolute attention and objective thinking. But it is only the C style individual who can do this day after day and not get tired of it. Not only that they don't get tired of it, but they also enjoy it and can think at deeper level than the other three styles due to their natural wiring to take their time to examine every angle and rely mostly on solid data (unlike the S and the I styles whose thinking is often tainted by feelings and emotions; or the D style whose thinking is interrupted by impulsive, gut decisions).

It is probably due to this ability of deep analytical thinking that many C style individuals also have great technical skills. They can operate certain software better than anyone around them, are able to troubleshoot and repair computers and other equipment, and/or have other great "handy" skills that require great attention to detail and extensive technical know-how.

Due to these great abilities of our C style friends, we often find ourselves turning to them whenever we need help with something that needs accuracy or precision; or when we need some help with a technical challenge, such as a computer problem or software usage "how to."

You'd definitely not run to your C style coworker or friend when you want to have some crazy fun-time – though you'll find plenty of high C style individuals in your environment who can be really humorous and fun to be around – but you'll definitely appreciate their presence in your life when you need help with something that needs accuracy and precision.

It also happens at times, that we don't fully appreciate the C individuals in our environment, due to their tendency to be almost invisible (when they are allowed to work on their tasks individually). We came to take it for granted that we get accurate and timely reports from them or we get great quality work from them, and we just accept that they are quiet and highly involved in their work.

I hope that after what you learned in the previous pages you got to have a higher appreciation for the C style individuals in your life. When you have a chance – hopefully today – walk over to your C style coworker (family member or friend) and tell them how much you appreciate the great work they are doing. (If you are an I style, resist the temptation to put your arm on their shoulder – C individuals love to keep a "polite" safe distance from others). Do not expect some great display of "Thank You – That's nice of you to say so…" emotional display. You might even get a slight frown; but trust me, they'll appreciate your display of appreciation of their outstanding work.

How to Motivate the C Style Individual

Regardless whether we are talking about an employee, child, a spouse, or significant other, there are a few simple ways to motivate these conscientious and detail-oriented individuals. While many of the suggestions below apply to motivating employees, several of the suggestions can be equally applied in other types of relationships as well.

- Speak to them in a more moderate pace, while sticking to the bottom line.
- *I need your expertise, We need your analytical abilities in order to succeed with this project,* and other similar statements have "magical" sound to the C style's ears and will often result in full engagement in the activity that needs completion
- Show them how something was successfully completed in the past - such as an instruction manual, training video, etc – they love the certainty of following well-established procedures.
- They like to feel a sense of certainty about what others expect of them. Let them know exactly what you want and what you do not want.
- Whenever possible provide upfront clear <u>written</u> instructions, rules, or procedures that will help them clearly understand what the expectations of them are.
- Assign them tasks that require the use of their analytical skills and their great abilities to pay attention to details.
- Allow them to work at their own pace and on their own or with other team-members who appreciate their strengths.

- Allow them enough time to complete their tasks and let them know by when you expect to see the results.
- Do not take them for granted! Praise them for a recent job that they completed successfully before assigning them new tasks.
- Enlist their help when planning a project or when planning implementation of major changes. Make sure that they are properly briefed on why those changes are necessary, otherwise they'll resist and even sabotage those changes. By letting them actively participate in the planning and implementation process, you'll get them as allies who'll facilitate the whole process with their full commitment.

Remember!
Motivating others can be "tricky." You can ONLY motivate people to do things they are interested in. Trying to motivate different styles to complete tasks that are totally against their behavioral tendencies can be futile and ineffective. Take the effort to recognize the behavioral style of the person who you are working with and motivate them by allowing them to capitalize on their natural strengths[1].

What Demotivates C Style Individuals

- High-speed environments can be a challenge for the high C style, especially if it involves operating in a change-rich environment and/or have to constantly meet tight deadlines.
- Uncertainty - tasks that require a great deal of guess-work can be stressful for the high C individual who prefers to follow well-established procedures and workflows.
- Uncertainty – not knowing what those around them expect of them.

---

[1] - Have your employee(s) take a DiSC® PPSS (or DiSC 2.0) to ensure that you get an accurate reading of the person's behavioral style. The DiSC profile will also suggest ways to motivate the person most effectively – for more details and to see a sample profile, visit **www.egSebastian.com/assessments**

- Social-interaction-rich environments can be a challenge for the high C, who'd rather prefer being able to work on their own on hands-on tangible tasks.
- Environments, jobs, or duties that require risk-taking.
- An environment where there are no clear rules to follow, or where coworkers constantly bend or break the rules
- Sudden changes in job description, work environment, work-flow, etc.
- Criticizing their work is a definite "no-no!" They've spent considerable time on producing the best outcome – you can't just walk in and criticize their output. If you do see a flaw in their work, politely and calmly ask questions that expose those flaws and see what they'll say. You'll find out that either your perception was wrong or they'll get right away on correcting the areas needing attention.
- If possible, do not pair them up to work with high I individuals. Of the four styles, the high I and high C styles are most likely not to get along and get easily into conflict. However, if both parties involved are trained in DISC, the likelihood that they'll get along and take advantage of each others' strengths is more likely.
- Working for a manager (or with a coworker) who talks fast and expects quick decisions. Only one thing can make this worse: if this manager (or coworker) also tends to be very humorous and talkative.

C Style Most Popular Career Choices[1]

Accountant	Accounting Clerk	Actuary
Administrative Assistant	Administrative Services Manager	Human Resources Manager**
Agricultural Engineer	Agricultural Scientist	Agricultural Worker
Air Traffic Controller	Aircraft Pilot	Aerospace Engineer
Artist and Related Careers***	Computer Hardware Engineers	Automotive Service Technician
Architect	Assembler	Astronomer
Athlete	Audiologist	Auditing Clerk
Auditor	School Principal**	Archivist
Barber	Bill Collector**	Billing Clerk
Biological Scientist	Biomedical Engineer	Bookkeeping Clerk
Civil Engineer	Brokerage Clerk	Budget Analyst
Bus Driver	Cartographer	Cashier
Chemical Engineer	Chemist	Chiropractor
Broadcast Engineering Technician	Appraisers and Assessors of Real Estate	Coin, Vending, and Amusement Machine Repairer
Clinical Laboratory Technologists	Clinical Laboratory Technician	Computer Programmer
Claims Adjuster	Appraiser	Examiner
Computer Repair	Computer Scientist	Auto Mechanic
Computer Support Specialist	Systems Administrator	Computer Software Engineer
Construction and Building Inspector	Construction Equipment Operator	Database Administrator

* - often in CS combination
** - often in CD combination
*** - often in CS or CSI combinations

---

[1] - in no particular order

Curator	Ballet Dancer	Data Entry
Cost Estimator	Dental Assistant	Dental Hygienist
Dental Laboratory Technician	Computer Systems Analyst	Conservation Scientist
Drywall Installer	Drafter	Economist
Education Administrator	Electrical and Electronics Engineer	Environmental Engineer
Electrician	Graphic Designer	Engineer
Dentist	Desktop Publisher	Financial Analyst
Farmer	Rancher	Management Analyst
Flight Engineer	Geological Engineer	Geoscientist
Physical Therapist Assistant and Aide	Environmental Scientist	Human Resources Assistant
Industrial Machinery Mechanic	Postal Service Worker	Information Processing Worker
Investigator**	Information Clerk	Lawyer**
Legal Assistant	Librarian	Library Assistant
Loan Officer	Loan Counselor	Mathematician
Manufacturing Engineer	Medical Laboratory Technician	Agricultural Manager**
Market Researcher**	Millwright**	Medical Scientist
Medical Transcriptionist	Occupational Health and Safety Specialist	Medical Records Technician
Mining Engineer	Judge**	Model
Mortician	Museum Technician	Musician
News Analyst	Nuclear Engineer	Meter Reader
Personal Financial Advisor	Office Machine Repairer	Operations Research Analyst
Dispensing Optician	Optometrist	Payroll Clerk

* - often in CS combination
** - often in CD combination
*** - often in CS or CSI combinations

Office Clerk	Pharmacist	Pharmacy Technician
Photogrammetrist	Plumber	Physical Therapist
Physician Assistant	Physician	Physicist
Electrical Installer and Repairer	Precision Instrument and Equipment Mechanic	Automotive Body and Related Repairer
Electronic Home Entertainment Equipment Installers and Repairer	Jewelers and Precious Stone and Metal Worker	Heating, Air-Conditioning, and Refrigeration Mechanic
Posting Clerk	Podiatrist	Prepress Technician
Respiratory Therapist	Private Detective**	Radiology Technician
Printing Machine Operator	Small Engine Mechanic	Sound Engineering Technician
Statistician	Surgeon	Surgical Technologist
Systems Analyst	Editor	Webmaster

* - often in CS combination

** - often in CD combination

*** - often in CS or CSI combinations

These are only a few of the careers most C style individuals tend to enjoy due to the many opportunities to work in environments where the daily routines give them plenty of chances to use their analytical, organizational, and other precision and accuracy related skills.

If your behavioral style blend contains two (or three) styles at about the same intensity[1] levels, remember to check the most popular career choices for your secondary style as well. If, for example, you are a CD style individual, you'll probably enjoy several of the careers listed in the *D's Most Popular Career Choices* on page 117.

---

[1] To get an accurate idea of what is your behavioral style, complete the valid and reliable DiSC® 2.0, DiSC 2Plus, or DiSC PPSS profile, at **www.egsebastian.com/disc_classic**

Important!

You probably noticed that the C style section contains more career choices than the other three styles. Fact is that many jobs and careers require great attention to detail and good organizational skills - all C style natural strengths. However, **anyone can perform most jobs** listed here or in any of the sections, and many of us do all the time. As most of our behavioral styles are a combination of two or more styles, many of us can easily reach into the strengths provided by our secondary or third style.

Just be careful not to choose a career that would require you to utilize behaviors that are totally opposite of your main style. For example, if you are a sky high I, you should not accept a position that require mostly C style behaviors; or C style should avoid jobs that requires mostly I style behaviors. The same applies to the D and S opposites.

Anyone can perform any job if they really want it; however, the level of job-satisfaction within each career could be dramatically reduced if the job-requirements are not in line with the person's natural behavioral tendencies.

For example, if a high I style individual gets a job as a data entry clerk or data analyst, this person will probably be able to do a fairly good job at it if he tries really hard; however, a) chances are that many mistakes will be made regularly and b) job-satisfaction will be minimal or none at all.

We spend one third of our entire life in our workplace – we owe it to ourselves to invest some effort to find the job/career that is most closely in line with our behavioral style. Use the suggested careers at the end of each chapter as a guide and choose wisely. Your job, after all, is one of the most important factors of your life. Choose wisely and you'll (potentially) have a great life; choose poorly and you'll most likely feel miserable most of the time – hopefully only at work, but fact is that many of us allow workplace frustrations to flow over into our personal lives.

Power Tip #6

Develop a deep appreciation for the C styles in your environment!

When it comes to communication, our society, for some reason, came to reward I style behaviors. It is expected from us to smile, be upbeat, humorous, and enthusiastic when we greet or talk to customers, friends, or family members. There are books and courses that teach people to display those behaviors in order to be more effective communicators. What we neglect to take in account, though, is that these behaviors do not come naturally to each style.

Due to their great attention to details and commitment to performing an excellent work, the C style individuals around you can come across as non-communicative and even anti-social at times... Keep in mind that this is happening because of their natural wiring, not because they do not like the people around them. And...

Realize that the C styles in your environment are often your greatest and often least appreciated "asset." They are the ones who make sure that tasks once started get completed, that everything is in its place, and everything that they work on get done accurately.

* Appreciate their strengths and accept their lower need to socialize (especially at work). Occasionally express your appreciation in words, praising their expertise, attention to detail, or whatever value you perceive that they provide to you, your workplace, or your family.

* Respect their need for quite time. C style individuals, at times, close up and want some time for themselves. Accept this need and do not take it personally – often there is nothing wrong, they just simply do exactly what they are supposed to do: they are following their inner wiring. (just like the other three style follow their natural wiring)

* Just think about it? Who do you want to be your surgeon, pilot, accountant, designer of sky scrapers, etc.? Be thankful for the C styles in your environment – we need their expertise badly!

Conscientiousness Style: *Improve Your Relationships and Effectiveness* **Self-Coaching Worksheet**
(Print out a blank self-coaching sheet at **www.egSebastian.com/selfcoach**)

1. What are my strengths that I'm most proud of?

_____

_____

_____

2. What are some of my strengths that make me most effective in my environment?

_____

_____

_____

3. What are some of my strengths that are (perhaps) perceived as weaknesses in my environment?

_____

_____

_____

4. What are some of my weaknesses that make me less effective in my environment?

_____

_____

_____

5. Based on what I read in this chapter (and on what I already knew), what
can I do to become more effective at creating and maintaining successful relationships in my workplace and/or at home? (Pages 199 - 204)

_____

_____

_____

_____

6. Based on what I read in this chapter (and on what I already knew), what can I do to become more effective at setting and accomplishing personal and professional goals? (Pages 199 - 204)

_____

_____

_____

_____

_____

_____

_____

7. Is it an option to speak to my supervisor (or coworkers) and ask to be assigned tasks that are more in line with my strengths? If yes, how would I approach him/her/them about it?

_____

_____

_____

_____

8. What else can I do to become more effective in all areas of my life? (Based on what you read – e.g., talk to spouse or significant other about your style and your style's needs, behavioral tendencies; how can you improve your relationship with loved ones, etc.)

_____

_____

_____

_____

_____

_____

_____

Chapter 8

The Four Styles at a Glance

The Four Styles at a Glance

There's no one on this planet who can call themselves an effective communicator without having at least a basic understanding of the four behavioral styles (or personality styles). Applying the Golden Rule – *Treat everyone the way you want to be treated* – is highly ineffective when it comes to communication and relationships . Instead, learning to apply the *people-smart rule,* that is *Treat everyone the way **they** want to be treated* is the key to building successful relationships; and this can be accomplished only with at least a basic understanding of different behavioral (or personality) styles.

This chapter provides you with a number of great at-a-glance visual illustrations of the four styles, helping you to easily get a better understanding of the general behavioral tendencies of each. To read more detail about any of the 4 styles, please visit Chapters 4 (D), 5 (I), 6 (S), and 7(C).

Table 9.1 – General characteristics of the four styles

	D	**I**	**S**	**C**
How to Recognize this Style?	Fast Paced & Task Oriented	Fast Paced & People Oriented	Moderate Paced & People Oriented	Moderate Paced & Task Oriented
General Behavioral Tendencies	Talks fast, moves fast, sticks to bottom line, loves to be in charge	Talks fast, moves fast, humorous, talkative, enthusiastic	Talks and moves at a more moderate pace; friendly, supportive, at times shy	Talks and moves at a more moderate pace; detail-oriented, analytical, formal
Main Strengths	Determined; makes things happen	Fun, friendly, enthusiastic	Supportive, loyal, great team player	Detail-oriented, thorough, accurate
	D	**I**	**S**	**C**

	D	I	S	C
Main Weaknesses	Blunt, easy to anger, dictatorial	Disorganized, over-promising, gossipy	Hesitant, shy, easily manipulated	Nitpicky, uncomuni-cative, resentful
Driven by Facts vs. Emotions	Facts	Emotions	Emotions	Facts
Main Focus	Setting goals, planning, getting the job done	Influencing and persuading others, building relationships, spreading optimism, entertaining self and others	Maintaining a safe and friendly environment; comfort (for self and others), teamwork	Planning and accurate execution of tasks
Can Come Across As	Blunt, insensitive, pushy, bossy, inpatient, stubborn	Impulsive, fake, disorganized, unrealistic, unreliable	Shy, slow, no initiative	Cold, slow, nitpicky, antisocial
Main Question	What?	Who?	*Why?*	*How?*
Under Pressure	Blunt, intolerant, demanding, reckless	Defensive, emotional, exaggerates and/or bluffs	Emotional, gives in/up easily	Defensive, blunt, indecisive, over-analyzing
Main Emotion	Anger	Enthusiasm and Optimism	Love and Staying Unemotio-nal	Worry
	D	I	S	C

	D	I	S	C
Biggest Energy Drains	Managed by or working side-by-side with slow, hesitant, and emotional people (S style)	Managed by or working with someone who is overly concerned about order, rules, and etiquette (C Style)	Managed by or working side by side with fast-paced, blunt, pushy, unsmiling people (D style)	Managed by or working side by side with fast-paced, chit-chatty, "funny," disorganized individuals (I style)
Fears	Loss of control, appearing weak,	Social rejection, appearance of incompe-tence, boredom	Sudden changes on the job, at home, etc., conflict	Criticism and non-appreciation of their work
Blind Spots	Blindly pushes own agenda and ideas on others	Interrupts and controls the conversation; poor listener, poor planner	Too agreeable, non-assertive, dependent	Too formal, overly critical, suspicious
Work "Style"	*Let me do it my way!*	*I want to do it the fun way*	*Show me how to do it the easy way*	*Let me do it the correct way*
Decision Making Process	Makes quick decisions and takes action immediately	Makes quick decisions; often procrasti-nates on taking action	Takes time to make a decision; might put off taking action for later, but once started she will follow through	Takes time to make a decision; analyzes all necessary data, plans a course of action, and follows plan closely
	D	I	S	C

General Behavioral Tendencies of the Four Styles

Fast Paced

AND

Dominance

- Dynamic
- Process-Driven
- Outspoken
- Wants to Control
- Practical
- Results Oriented
- Bottom Line
- Decisive

Can come across as

- Bossy
- Inconsiderate
- Inpatient
- Aggressive

Influence

- Enthusiastic
- Talkative
- Persuasive
- Entertaining
- Easygoing
- Relationship-Driven
- Involved
- Humorous

Can come across as

- Impulsive
- Disorganized
- Tiring
- Fake

AND

Task Oriented

OR

People Oriented

Conscientiousness

- Cautious
- Organized
- Analytical
- Thorough
- Quality-Driven
- Accurate
- Dependable
- Formal

Can come across as

- Distant
- Perfectionist
- Nitpicky
- Antisocial

Steadiness

- Supportive
- Friendly
- Considerate
- Humble
- Cooperative
- Stability-Driven
- Great Listener
- Calm

Can come across as

- Slow
- Passive
- Hesitant / Shy
- Easily Manipulated

AND

Moderate Paced

AND

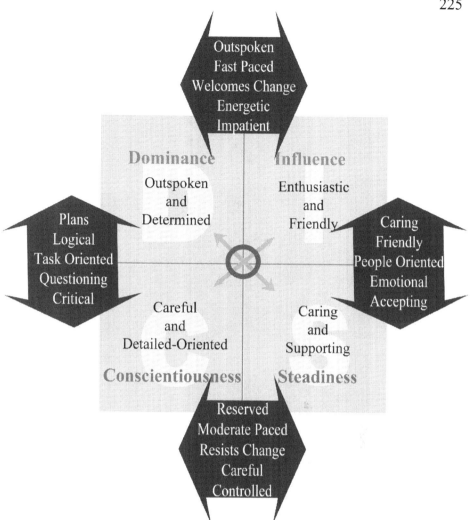

Figure 9.1 – Visual depiction of common characteristics of the four styles   (highlighted in black)

Common Characteristics of the Styles

As we explored the four main behavioral styles, you had a chance to observe the vast differences among the styles. The good news is, that each style has something in common with two adjacent styles. Figure 9.2 gives you a good visual depiction, while Table 9.2 provides a more detailed description of the common elements o f the four styles.

Fast Paced[1] Individuals Tend to be...	Moderate Paced[2] Individuals Tend to be...
• Active • Outgoing • Optimistic • Great Starter • Poor Finisher • Energetic • Impulsive • Involved • Positive • Enthusiastic • Tradition Breaker • Dislikes Routine Tasks • Likes To Bend the Rules • Outspoken • Welcomes Change	• Worrisome • Poor Starter • Great Finisher • Reserved • Careful • Hesitant • Calm • Conservative • Controlled • Likes Routine Tasks • Follows Rules • Resists Change • Expect Others to Guess their Thoughts and Expectations
Task Oriented[3] **Individuals Tend to be...**	**People Oriented[4]** **Individuals Tend to be...**
• Questioning • Distant • Logical • Critical • Likes to Plan • Analytical • Focused • Process-Oriented • Unemotional	• Accepting • Friendly • Talkative • Humorous • Caring • People Pleaser • Easy Going • Relationships-Driven • Displays Emotions

Table 9.2 – Common characteristics of the four styles

---

[1] - Dominance (D) and Influence (I)
[2] - Steadiness (S) and Conscientiousness (C)
[3] - Conscientiousness (C) and Dominance (D)
[4] - Steadiness (S) and Influence (I)

Strengths of the Four Styles

Fast Paced

Task Oriented / **People Oriented**

Dominance

- Goal and achievement driven
- Believes in self (confident)
- Determined
- Independent
- Quick decision maker
- Takes charge and makes things happen
- Pragmatic thinker
- Effective planner
- Focused and productive
- Has high risk tolerance
- Tenacious
- Outspoken and fearless
- Great problem solver
- Competitive

Influence

- People person
- Passionate and enthusiastic
- Persuasive
- Friendly and caring
- Entertaining
- Curious
- Independent
- Creative and innovative
- Quick decision maker
- Compassionate
- Helpful
- Optimistic
- Spontaneous
- Smiling and kind
- Great at defusing conflict

OR

Conscientiousness

- Great self-control
- Detail oriented
- Accurate
- Thorough
- Questioning
- Sticks to facts and figures
- Modest
- Diplomatic
- Plans and schedules most activities
- Reliable
- Great problem solver
- Fair listener
- Focused
- Systematic

Steadiness

- Great listener
- Patient and careful
- Trusting and trustworthy
- Respectful – will try hard not to hurt others' feelings
- Supportive
- Great follower
- They finish what they start
- Consistent, reliable, and dependable
- Does not mind routine work
- Loyal (both to her workplace and relationships
- Cooperative; great team-player

Moderate Paced

Challenge Areas of the Four Styles

Fast Paced

Task Oriented • **People Oriented**

Dominance

- Pushy and dictatorial
- Often disregards others opinions and input
- Blunt and inconsiderate
- Poor listener – interrupts when others talk
- Challenges authority
- Challenges the status quo
- Fault finding
- Has difficulty delegating
- Stubborn
- Impatient
- They believe they are always right
- Impulsive and reckless
- Aggressive

Influence

- Talks too much
- Over promising
- Gossipy
- Talks in superlatives
- Exaggerates; at times fibs
- Poor listener
- Interrupts when others talk
- Emotional
- Easily distracted
- Impulsive and undisciplined
- Scatter-minded
- Permissive
- Irresponsible
- Unpredictable
- Disorganized

OR

Conscientiousness

- Perfectionist
- Nitpicky
- Hard-to-please
- Worrisome
- Uncommunicative
- Unsmiling
- Emotionally non-expressive
- Unforgiving
- Resentful
- Rigid
- Suspicious
- Untrusting
- Too formal
- Unrealistically high expectations of everyone

Steadiness

- Hesitant & shy
- Dependent
- Easily manipulated
- To avoid conflict, puts on a "non-emotional mask" and will not verbalize challenges
- Has difficulty being assertive; afraid to hurt others' feelings
- Passionately dislikes changes
- Bases decisions on emotions
- Worrisome
- Passive
- Sensitive
- Naïve

Moderate Paced

Communication Tendencies of the Four Styles

Fast Paced

AND

Dominance

- Talks Fast
- Poor listener
- Factual
- Direct
- Pushy
- Logical
- Does not like to listen to emotional outbursts
- Questioning
- Task-oriented
- Bottom-line focused
- Easy-to-anger
- Likes to take action vs. talking about taking action

AND

Influence

- Fast-talker
- Poor listener
- Easygoing
- Open-book
- Verbose
- Entertaining
- Openly expresses emotions
- Talks in stories
- Talks in superlatives
- Enthusiastic
- Persuasive
- Likes to brainstorm and will offer help to problem-solve
- Likes to talk about taking action

Task Oriented

People Oriented

OR

Conscientiousness

- Talks at a moderate pace
- Detail and task oriented
- Questioning
- Sticks to facts and figures
- Controlled
- Diplomatic
- Introverted and withdrawn
- Dry and brief when socializing
- Can be verbose when describing technical details
- Hesitant when required to make quick decisions
- Fair listener
- Judgmental

Steadiness

- Talks at a moderate pace
- Patient
- Great listener
- Friendly and easygoing
- Respectful and considerate
- Non-confrontational
- Openly expresses emotions in friendly conversations
- Controls emotions in order to avoid conflict
- Thoughtful
- Great ability to empathize
- Indecisive and hesitant when making major decisions
- Shy (at times)
- Humble

AND

AND

Moderate Paced

What the Four Styles Expect of You

AND

Dominance

- *Don't bother me, unless you have something important to say*
- *Be brief when approaching me*
- *Don't waste my time with humor or stories*
- *Respect my high drive and need for accomplishment*
- *Be honest; lay it out as it is – don't bundle up things*
- *Listen well to what I'm saying; I don't like to repeat myself*
- *Take initiative – just do it!*

AND

Influence

- *Please smile when you approach me, talk to me, and when I talk to you*
- *If you have a problem with me, let's discuss it – do not lecture me nor yell at me*
- *Listen to my stories and jokes and laugh with me*
- *When working on a project, <u>show</u> me step-by-step what to do and how to do it*
- *Be upbeat and relaxed around me*
- *I like public recognition - praise me often*

Task Oriented

OR

People Oriented

Conscientiousness

- *When you talk to me, stick to facts and data*
- *Be brief and to the point*
- *Be prepared! Know what you are talking about*
- *Avoid stories, jokes, and other non-work related chit-chat*
- *Please , no expressing feelings, sentiments, and emotions*
- *Don't rush me*
- *Don't dump sudden changes on me*
- *If you work close to me, please do not be messy, loud, late, or sloppy*

Steadiness

- *Be patient and friendly*
- *Do not shout at me!*
- *Smile*
- *Do not push me – let me do things at my own pace*
- *Understand and respect the fact that I'm more in touch with my feelings than the other three styles*
- *Please do not use sarcasm when you talk to me*
- *Listen to what I have to say*
- *Do not dump sudden changes on me*

AND

AND

Can Improve Performance And Relationships by...

Fast Paced

Dominance

- Slow down
- Plan your tasks and pay more attention to details
- Consider consequences before you jump into something
- Take the effort to listen better (see pg. 42)
- Criticize less
- Praise good performers
- Consider others feelings
- Listen to others' input
- Stop trying to control everyone around you
- Learn to control your anger
- Smile more

Influence

- Talk less; listen more (pg. 42)
- Talk less; do more
- Stop talking about yourself; take conscious effort to listen to what others have to say
- Write your goals and tasks down and develop a course of action
- Use a planner – stick to the plan
- Commit to working on one task at a time
- Commit to finishing what you start
- Under-promise & over-deliver
- Get and stay organized

OR

Conscientiousness

- Relax your obsession with order and rules - just a bit; especially drop your expectation of others being as organized as you – it is not everyone's priority to be so particular about order
- Learn about the other three styles and try to raise your acceptance of each; learn to appreciate their strengths
- Show more empathy – respect others feelings and needs
- Speed up a bit, when possible
- Smile

Steadiness

- Speed up whenever quality will not suffer as a result
- Learn to say "No" (pg. 296)
- Practice expressing your needs and verbalize your hurts; do it without coming across as complaining, but rather bringing attention to what might be unfair or unjust practices around you
- Practice assertiveness
- Take initiative when you see that something needs to be done, even if you think that it's not your duty

Moderate Paced

Task Oriented | **People Oriented**

AND

Learning Styles of the Four Behavioral Styles

Fast Paced

AND

Dominance

- Likes to hear bottom line information
- Learns best through being exposed to valid data and logic-based information
- When in a learning environment, might blurt out questions during class (will not raise hands unless [repeatedly] asked to do so)
- Enjoys hands-on, practical ways of learning, such as "learn it while you do it"
- Often learns through trial-and-error

AND

Influence

- Learns best through listening to stories and anecdotes
- Can get frustrated when exposed to too much data
- Will interrupt instructor with questions (will not raise hands unless [repeatedly] asked to do so)
- Learning is best anchored when has a chance to do hands-on activities
- Tries to make the learning process entertaining and fun

Task Oriented

OR

People Oriented

Conscientiousness

- Likes a formal & scheduled learning environment
- Learns best through exposure to raw data, statistics, and other logic-based bottom-line information
- Enjoys – and needs – to hear in-depth coverage of technical subjects
- Will raise hand to ask questions or make comments
- Needs opportunity to discuss areas that might need further clarification

Steadiness

- Learns best through listening to stories and anecdotes, combined with some data, statistics, etc.
- Needs to hear in-depth how-to information and ideally get a chance to do some hands-on practice
- Could be shy to ask all questions that pop into her mind
- Will always raise hand to pose a question or comment
- Patient and thorough learner

AND

AND

Moderate Paced

How to Communicate Effectively with the Four Styles

Fast Paced

Dominance

When approaching a high D:

- Don't waste their time
- Keep your conversation short and focused on the topic at hand
- Stay away from jokes and stories (especially at work)
- Show your competence early in the conversation
- Allow them to feel in charge

For the D style subordinate: Provide clear rules and <u>firm expectations</u>

Influence

When approaching a high I:

- Smile and be informal
- Use humor and share personal (or not –so personal) anecdotes
- Praise them for their accomplishments
- Listen to their stories and jokes
- Allow them to express their feelings
- Whenever possible, don't bore them with too much technicalities and details

For the I style subordinate: Provide them with written details of what's expected & <u>regularly follow up on their progress</u>

OR

Conscientiousness

When approaching a high C:
- Use short sentences and stick to the bottom line
- Stay away from jokes and stories (especially at work)
- Show your competence early in the conversation
- Don't criticize their work (ask related questions instead)
- Display appreciation for detail & accuracy

For the C style subordinate: Provide deadlines (as they want to do an excellent job, they at times take too much time)

Steadiness

When approaching a high S:
- Smile
- Exercise patience: don't rush them
- Give them a chance/time to express themselves
- Express your appreciation of their work, etc.
- Don't push them to go beyond their comfort zone (whenever possible)

For the S style subordinate: Provide clear and detailed description of job related duties & provide detailed reasons for upcoming changes

Moderate Paced

Task Oriented

People Oriented

The Four Styles at Work

Fast Paced

AND

Dominance

- High energy
- Action and result oriented
- Enjoys challenges
- Makes quick decisions
- Great problem solver
- Takes initiative
- Handles conflict assertively and on the spot
- Wants to do things his way
- Challenges the status-quo
- Challenges authority
- Bossy / Pushy
- Irritable
- Likes to bend the rules
- Wants immediate results

AND

Influence

- Helpful
- Enjoys interacting with coworkers and clients
- Generates enthusiasm
- Injects "fun" into everything
- Loves to persuade
- Creative
- Loves small group teams
- Loves to be praised
- Takes initiative
- Over-promising
- Expressive
- Habitual procrastinator
- Disorganized
- Likes to bend rules

Task Oriented

People Oriented

OR

Conscientiousness

- Follows rules closely
- Loves to develop and / or follow procedures
- Organized and a great planner
- Focuses heavily on accuracy
- Objective thinker
- Pays attention to details
- Systematic and careful
- Expects quality work from others
- Does not like to socialize while working
- Introspective
- Low risk tolerance
- Judgmental

Steadiness

- Follows rules
- Likes to support others
- Likes easy-to-complete tasks
- Likes a predictable environment
- Great listener
- Dependable
- Works at steady pace
- Has great follow-through
- Patient
- Calm and smiling
- Loyal
- Hesitant
- Does not express hurts
- Sensitive
- Resists – and might sabotage - change

AND

AND

Moderate Paced

How to Motivate the Four Styles

Fast Paced

AND

Dominance

- **Control** - Let them feel in complete charge of projects!
- **Change** - Give them challenging tasks
- **Power** - Provide them with authority over team-members
- **Results** - Provide plenty of opportunities for accomplishment
- Set tangible rewards for accomplishing goals, such as advancement opportunities, financial rewards, etc.

AND

Influence

- **Popularity** – give them opportunities to shine
- **Approval** – express your satisfaction with their performance
- **Relationships** – allow them to work in environments where they can utilize their excellent people skills
- **Recognition** – provide public recognition for outstanding performance
- "It will be fun," "I know you can do this – you are good at this," and similar statements are music to their ears

Task Oriented

People Oriented

OR

Conscientiousness

- **Logic** – provide opportunities that allows them to create something - or solving problems - with the use of logic and their analytical skills
- **Certainty** – create an environment that feels stable; one where they can apply their technical skills and <u>know</u> that they'll get the expected results
- **Expertise** – express your appreciation for their knowledge and expertise
- Do not rush them; allow them to work at their own pace
  - Ask for their input before implementing changes

Steadiness

- Smile when you talk to them
- **Security** – provide a sense of a stable, unchanging, and safe environment
- **Harmony** – ability to develop and follow routines; creating and maintaining successful relationships
- **Relationships** – ability to spend time supporting others
- **Appreciation** - they want to feel a sense of belonging and appreciation
- Do not rush them; and give them plenty of time to prepare for upcoming changes

AND

AND

Moderate Paced

What Demotivates the Four Styles at Work

Fast Paced

Task Oriented

People Oriented

AND

Dominance

- A micro-managing manager or supervisor
- A slow, hesitant manager
- Needing to report on every move they make
- Monotonous work
- A slow environment that's void of opportunities for overcoming challenges and has no rewards for the **D**'s competitive and fast-paced nature
- Working side-by side with unmotivated, slow paced, and talkative people

Influence

- A slow, analytical micro-manager who is overly concerned about minuscule details, order, and rules
- Routine activities
- Monotonous tasks (especially if it does not involve social interaction)
- Tasks that require too much analytical or technical skills
- Working around hostile and negative people
- Not being listened to
- Lack of opportunities for quick accomplishments

OR

Conscientiousness

- High speed environments
- Working for high speed, humorous, and unfocused manager
- Working around talkative, pushy, or overly humorous people
- Criticism of their work
- Uncertainty – a job that has no predictability on what type of tasks are to be completed
- Not knowing what those around them expect of them
- Sudden, unexpected changes in job description, environment, etc

Steadiness

- Unexpected and major – or not so major – changes that affect their daily routines
- Regular conflict
- Tight deadlines
- High speed, challenge-rich environments
- Working around negative and hostile people
- Working for a blunt, fast-paced, and demanding manager
- Not feeling appreciated

Moderate Paced

How to Manage the Four Styles

Fast Paced

Task Oriented

People Oriented

Dominance

AND

- Let them feel in charge of projects
- Be firm – if they sense weakness on your part, they'll end up running the show
- When working as part of a team, give them authority to lead
- Do not try to motivate them through stories;
- Don't waste their time with humor
- They are motivated self-starters – simply tell them what to do, and they'll do it

Influence

AND

- Give them opportunities to use their persuasive skills
- They feel disrespected if you don't listen to their stories and humor – make them happy occasionally by listening to their "chatter"
- Provide them with <u>clear deadlines and instructions</u> **in writing**
- Smile and be friendly when you talk to them
- Regularly <u>follow up</u> on their progress, as they have a strong tendency to procrastinate

OR

Conscientiousness

- Keep your conversation brief and focused to the bottom line
- Refrain from personal stories, jokes, or anecdotes
- Show competence
- Don't criticize their work; instead ask questions related to the area that seems questionable to you
- Show your appreciation for their attention to detail and accuracy
- Give them clear deadlines (or they'll work forever on their tasks, trying to attain perfection)

Steadiness

- Understand that they feel most comfortable when following a routine
- Give them a <u>clear</u> job description – they'll usually follow it closely but will not go beyond it
- Allow them to express themselves fully; if you interrupt, you might never find out what they had to say
- Smile when you talk and listen
- Inform them in a timely manner about upcoming changes
- Express your appreciation of their great work

AND

AND

Moderate Paced

How to Communicate Effectively with Your D, I, S, or C Style Manager

Fast Paced

Task Oriented

People Oriented

AND

AND

AND

AND

OR

Dominance

- You have an inpatient, results-driven manager - don't waste her time with chit-chat
- Be ready to hear your boss raise her voice and be blunt at times
- Understand that your boss's anger and outbursts are not personal
- Abstain from sharing personal stories and jokes
- Stick to the bottom line
- Show competence
- Show your ability to make quick decisions and take action immediately

Influence

- You have an amiable, enthusiastic, talkative, and potentially somewhat disorganized manager
- Take some time to listen to her jokes and stories and laugh freely when appropriate
- Feel free to occasionally share some of your stories and jokes
- Praise them for their great (and not so great) accomplishments
- Help your manager plan things – she is somewhat impulsive – she needs your help
- Support your manager with your organizational skills

Conscientiousness

- You have a cautious, analytical, and somewhat of a perfectionist manager
- Stick to the bottom line
- Do not tell stories, nor use humor in your conversation
- Be prepared – know what you are talking about
- Do not criticize your manager's ideas, projects, etc. – she put into it hours or weeks of thinking; instead ask questions that will help you understand the puzzling areas
- Match your manager's more moderate speech rate

Steadiness

- You have a supportive, kind, and a bit cautious manager
- Take your time – do not rush when explaining something – give them plenty of details
- Expect a cautious, slow decision making process
- Be prepared to listen carefully; they usually think before they speak and they often need to muster enough courage to express themselves
- Do not interrupt them when they speak
- Praise them regularly for accomplishments

Moderate Paced

D, I, S, and C Style Customers' Expectations of You

Fast Paced

Dominance

- *Give me the bottom line on your product or service*
- *Be knowledgeable and professional*
- *Don't waste my time with humor or stories*
- *Listen well to what I have to say– I don't like to repeat myself, nor do I always have the patience for it*
- *Understand that patience is not one of my strengths*
- *Don't try to manipulate me – I'm allergic to scams*
- *Be confident & Speak up!*

Influence

- *Please smile when you approach me and talk to me, as well as when I talk to you*
- *Understand that it's important for me to break the ice through humor or humorous short stories.*
- *Listen to my stories and jokes and laugh with me*
- *Be upbeat and relaxed around me*
- *Give me plenty of options*
- *Show some enthusiasm*
- *Don't overwhelm me with too much technical details*

OR

Conscientiousness

- *I like to keep our conversation formal*
- *When you talk to me, stick to facts and data*
- *Be brief and to the point*
- *Be prepared! Know what you are talking about*
- *I need in-depth details in order to bring a decision*
- *Avoid stories, jokes, and other non-topic related chit-chat*
- *Don't rush me and try to speak at a more moderate pace*
- *Give me plenty of time to think*

Steadiness

- *Be patient and friendly*
- *Smile*
- *Do not push me! Do not use hard selling tactics on me – I get intimidated by that*
- *Give me several options, give me enough details on them, then give me time to think*
- *I like time-tested and proven products that are easy to use*
- *Listen carefully to what I have to say – I'll often <u>not</u> express my needs if I'm not encouraged to speak*

Task Oriented

People Oriented

AND

Moderate Paced

How to Defuse Conflict with the Four Styles

(See pages 112, 144, 172, and 206 for more details)

Fast Paced

Task Oriented

People Oriented

Dominance

AND

- Run! You can't win. This is a behavioral style that can really *blow the lid off* and will fight like a tiger. Make sure to <u>wait till they calm down.</u>
- Let them vent – they will get more upset if you interrupt them
- .Do not lose your temper, nor give in to them
- Use non-emotional language
- When giving your side of the story, <u>stay calm,</u> appeal to their logic; and <u>use brief sentences loaded with facts</u>

Influence

AND

- Understand that they do not like conflict
- Be prepared for emotional outbursts
- Allow them to vent – listen to their side of the story - then ask them "if we can discuss the issue in a calm manner"
- Validate their emotions: "I understand <u>why</u> this makes you upset, but let's take a look at the facts and let's see how we can come up with a solution
- <u>Have them repeat what you agreed upon</u>

OR

Conscientiousness

- Will often carry on grudges for months or years without the other person ever knowing why a tension is there between the two
- Encourage them to open up and speak freely
- Avoid raising your voice
- Even if their reasoning sounds unreasonable, validate: say "I'm sorry to hear that xyz made you feel that way. Let's try to come up with a solution that will be a win-win for both of us."
  - <u>Quote rules and regulations whenever possible</u>

AND

Steadiness

- They are often unaware of the existence of a conflict – break it to them in a calm, friendly manner
- On their side, conflict can often go on undetected due to their tendency to hide their hurts and negative emotions
- Encourage them to talk
- Listen without interrupting
- Understand that they will do everything in their power to defuse the conflict themselves
- Do not raise your voice
- Validate their "pain"; suggest to work out a solution together

AND

Moderate Paced

Celebrity DISC Styles

Fast Paced

AND

Dominance

- Martin Luther King
- Hilary Rodham Clinton
- Harrison Ford
- Madonna (the singer)
- Denzel Washington
- Robert De Niro
- Al Pacino
- Joe Pesci

AND

Influence

- Bill Clinton (ID Style)
- Whoopi Goldberg
- Robin Williams
- Edie Murphy
- Ellen DeGeneres
- Jim Carrey
- Jay Leno
- Katie Couric

Task Oriented

OR

People Oriented

Conscientiousness

- Bill Gates
- Al Gore
- Martha Stuart
- Jenifer Aniston, in the movie *The Break-Up*
- Steve Martin, in *Shopgirl*
- Robin Williams, in *Final Cut*
- Dan Acroid in Dragnet
- Sandra Bullock
- Dr. Ben Bernanke, Fed Chairman

Steadiness

- Mahatma Gandhi
- Barbara Bush
- John Denver
- Forest Whitaker
- Meg Ryan (in her early movies)
- Tim Russert
- President Jimmy Carter
- Jesus Christ (most likely SDC combination)

AND

AND

Moderate Paced

Remember!

The information in this chapter is broken down to the bare basics in order to give you an easy-to-view DISC-in-action tools; to read more about any of the areas covered in this chapter, look up the specific areas that you are interested in Chapters 4 (Dominance), 5 (Influence), 6 (Steadiness) and 7 (Conscientiousness).

For example, if you want to read more on how to deal with conflict with a Conscientiousness (C) style individual, you'd look up Chapter 7 and look for *How to Deal with Conflict when Dealing with a C Style Individual.* Use the Table of Contents at the beginning of the book for easier navigation.

Power Tip #8

Increase your acceptance of everyone around you!

Effective communication – and as a result, successful relationships – are only possible if you learn to accept those around you unconditionally. To accomplish this, get a good understanding of the behavioral tendencies of the four styles; then as you go through your days interacting with others, notice each person's behavioral style and instead of judging others, stressing about differences, or even worse, getting into conflict with others, simply notice a person's style and realize that most of their behaviors are 100% as normal as your behaviors, except they are wired with a different focus of what matters and how to approach what matters.

When you master the "art" of unconditional acceptance of those around you, that's when you'll start being perceived as a "master" communicator, and a great person that everyone will enjoy being around.

Author's Last Note

"Most relationships are not made in heaven. They come in kits and you have to put them together yourself."

- Anonymous -

Creating a More Peaceful World One Person at a Time...

In 2003 I participated in a 4-hour DISC seminar and it changed the dynamics of all my relationships. I'm saying this without any exaggeration: DISC has made me a much better person – a more peaceful and understanding being; I became a much better husband, parent, son, coach/consultant – and a much more effective communicator in general with everyone around me.

I believe that DISC can have the same effect on you and anyone who takes the effort to learn these concepts. I truly believe that through my efforts, the efforts of other DISC trainers, and through your efforts to spread the DISC concepts, we can create a more peaceful world one person at a time...

In the past 5 years, I attempted to affect others' lives the same way as mine was affected by the first DISC seminar I attended. By the date of publishing this book, I have helped thousands of people improve their communication skills, and people skills in general, through my workshops, seminars, coaching, teleclasses, eCourses, and my audio and video programs.

I truly believe that simply by attempting to better understand those around us, will raise our acceptance levels of everyone and will dramatically reduce stress and conflict that was originally present due to the lack of understanding of the behaviors of those who surround us.

In the past, I used to judge people from the "box" of my personality style, expecting everyone to be just like me – enthusiastic, smiling, friendly, easy-going, chatty, etc., etc. – so, so many unrealistic expectations... Through DISC I learned that we are all different IN VERY PREDICTABLE WAYS, and through that predictability I could easily recognize different personality – or behavioral styles – around me and understand WHY some people were so dramatically different from me. But, unlike in the past, now I welcome these differences and I experience dramatically reduced (almost none) frustration, stress, and conflict with those around me.

I hope that this book will serve you – or already has served you - as a catalyst in improving your communication skills and your relationships.

If you have found these concepts useful and want to share a DISC success story, please email it to me to **eg@egSebastian.com**, with DISC SUCCESS STORY in the subject line. <u>With your permission</u> I will publish your story on my website or in other upcoming publications.

Thank you for taking the time to read my book and I hope to meet you in person at one of my future live events…

and...

…the beginning of better communication and improved relationships, right?

About the Author

E   G   Sebastian – America's Peaceful Communication Messenger - is a dynamic speaker who never fails to keep his audience engaged with his high value presentations, humor, and interaction with the participants. His years of management experience, linked with his more than 15-years experience as a motivator and personal coach, make him the speaker of choice for programs related to personal & professional growth.

E.G. is available to speak internationally. He speaks six languages and presents in four: English, Spanish, Hungarian, and Romanian.

E.G.'s fascination with Effective Communication began at an early age. He grew up in a cult-like environment where as a child he faced countless restrictions. He was not allowed to have friends who were not of his family's faith (which there were none in his neighborhood), was restricted to listening only religious music, and he was physically and verbally abused almost on a daily basis[1].

As a result of his strict upbringing, he developed some very poor social skills and spent his childhood feeling alienated from his classmates and the other children in his neighborhood. He'd spend his days watching other children play and wonder how they were able to play so freely; and wondered why he (E.G.) was not able to join them and enjoy their company. During this period – ages 7 to 17 – he'd resolve most of his verbal misunderstandings with fist-fights, which got him in trouble quite often.

He started reading books on psychology, self-improvement, and effective communication at the early age of nine, and in the following years he became a regular at the city library and read all the books that he could put his hands on in these topics. By his twenties he read literally hundreds of books on the topic of self-improvement.)

*

By today, E.G. is happily married and has three children – Alexandra 12, Philip 11, and Adriana-Bianca 1 – and he prides himself in having a super-successful marriage, where arguments and raised voice is a very rare occurrence. He also broke the chain of abuse. It is said that abused children will become abusive parents, but E.G. took control of his "dark side" and

---

[1] - At age 14 the physical abuse suddenly stopped and in the following years E.G. developed a great relationship with his parents. Presently E.G.'s parents are the best grandparents any grandchild could dream about.

raises his kids with no spanking or other type of physical or verbal abuse. Furthermore he is very proud of the fact that he spends hours of quality time with his family every week, rollerblading, swimming, hiking, biking, camping, playing music together, and all kind of other activities that he engages into in order to keep a strong relationship with his children and wife.

Both E.G.'s wife and his children are proficient in the "language" of DISC, which helps them understand each other better and communicate with one another based on each family member's behavioral style.

E.G.'s professional career started in 1990, at age 23, as an interpreter – Hungarian/English/German/Romanian/Chinese, helping foreign investors set up their companies in Hungary; then in 1991 he became the general manager and 49% owner of a Chinese-Hungarian joint venture - an export-import company - which he successfully managed till 1995. In the following years, E.G. shifted his career into his area of passion: communication & leadership development coaching and public speaking.

E.G. is the past area governor - for two consecutive years - of Toastmasters International, a non-profit organization that helps individuals develop public speaking and leadership skills He has a bachelor's degree in business management, is a certified empowerment coach, a certified seminar leader (though the American Seminar Leaders Association), and is an Inscape Certified DiSC Behavioral System Trainer/Facilitator.

Works Cited

1. Steven Covey, *Seven Habits of Highly Effective People.* Simon and Schuster, 1989

2. Sun Tzu, *The Art of War.* Shambhala, 2005

3. Martin E.P. Seligman et. Al., Abnormal Psychology. W.W. Norton & Company, Inc., 2001

4. William Moulton Marston, *The Emotions of Normal People,* London: Kegan Paul 1928. (International Library of Psychology, Philosophy and Scientific Method)

APPENDIX A

Invite E.G. Sebastian to speak at your next event!

Let E.G. energize and entertain your group, while providing high quality information. E.G.'s presentations often include magic and plenty of humor, while also energizing his audiences with a multitude of group activities and self-discovery activities.

Visit **www.egsebastian.com/events_calendar** for a list of upcoming events

**For date availability and for more information
please call Toll Free at 877 379-3793
or send eMail to eg@egSebastian.com**

Here are some of the DiSC®[1]-based topics E.G. presents:
- **Performance**
  - Maximizing Your Strengths as a Manager
  - Recognizing and Removing Your Employees' Barriers to Performance
  - How to Motivate Your Employees - Getting the Most from Your Key Contributors

- **Communication**
  - Different People, Different Needs – Improve Your Customer Service through Better Understanding their Needs
  - Communication Skills Magic – Improve Your Personal & Professional Relationships
  - Understanding and Adapting to Different Behavioral Styles

- **Conflict**
  - Managing Conflict and Resistance
  - How to Deal with Difficult Coworkers/Customers

- **Interpersonal**
  - Understanding and Using Your Strengths to Your Advantage
  - Improve Your Confidence & Communication Skills by Building Greater Self-Awareness

---

[1] - DiSC® with lower case "i" is an Inscape Publishing, Inc trademark

APPENDIX A – Continued…

- **Sales**
  - Building a Sales Relationship
  - How to be More Responsive to Customer Differences

- **Team**
  - Improving Team Effectiveness
  - Improving Team Motivation

- **Coaching Skills Training** (for managers, social workers, and counselors)
  - Understanding Your Clients'/Employees' Needs
  - Tools & Techniques to Coach Your Employees to Increased On-the-Job Effectiveness
  - Tools & Techniques to Coach Your Clients to more personal & professional success

- **Stress Management**
  - 12 Effective Stress Management Techniques in a Fast-Paced World

Keynotes

For Adult & Youth Events

- How to Create a More Peaceful World One Person at a Time
- Your Success Story Starts Today!
- The 7 Building Blocks of Success
- Your Attitude Determines Your Altitude
- Leadership in the New Milenium
- Communication is More than Just Talk
- Transform Your Life into a Work of Art

APPENDIX B

Performance/Leadership Development Coaching/Mentoring

Would you like to improve your leadership skills? Or... do you have employees or managers who are not performing to their full potential?

E.G. Sebastian provides performance and leadership development coaching to help you maximize your performance and leadership skills:

- learn about your behavioral style's strengths and weaknesses
- discover your behavioral style's "natural" barriers to top performance in your field
- get coached to brake your "natural barriers to top performance
- learn to easily recognize your subordinates' behavioral styles
- learn how to communicate most effectively with employees and managers of different behavioral styles
- explore simple yet powerful ways to motivate your employees most effectively
- discover how to deal with – and even prevent - conflict with employees or managers of different styles
- raise your awareness of your weaknesses and gain control over them
- improve your overall performance by learning how to capitalize on your strengths

Behind every successful individual there is a coach or a mentor
Take your leadership skills to the next level!

90 Days Money-Back Guarantee!

You either notice <u>considerable results</u> in your
performance and communication skills,
or you get 100% refund!

Call Toll Free 877 379-3793 for more information,
or inquire by email at **support@egSebastian.com**

APPENDIX C

– Volume Discount –
Communication-Skills Magic

Communication-Skills Magic **– Volume Discount Prices:**

10 to 50 copies - $13.97

51 to 100   - $11.97

101 to 500   - $9.97

500 to 1000   - $8.97

1000+ copies   - $7.97

For more information, please call Toll Free 877 379-3793

APPENDIX D

7 Ways to Say "NO"
Without Hurting Others' Feelings

For two of the styles – the D and C styles - saying "NO" comes rather naturally. They are so focused on moving towards completing their tasks – or towards their goals – that they can care less of how a "NO" would affect others' feelings. They are pretty good at interrupting chit-chatty coworkers, clients, etc. and are great at accomplishing whatever they set their mind to.

However, two of the stiles – the I and the S (and especially the S style) – have great concern for others' feelings; therefore they often say yes to things that they would rather not do. Even when they have a full schedule and someone asks for a favor, they most often will say "YES."

Things to consider:
1. **What** do you say "NO" to, when you say "YES" to things that you don't want to do?
Whenever you say "yes" just to please those around you, you say "NO" to things that matter to you, such as completing your tasks, self-care, spending more time with your family, etc.
2. What message do you send if you say "yes" to most people that ask for favors, or simply regularly abuse your time by demanding a listening ear?
That you are helpful and kind? Maybe… That you are easily manipulated… That you are not assertive… Think about it!
3. When you say "yes" to things that you don't really want to do, you disrespect both yourself and the other person; and in the long run you'll probably develop resentment against the other person. To avoid this, respect yourself and the other person by learning to say "NO."
4. Saying "YES" too often, just to please those around you, will very likely lead to unnecessary stress and possibly burnout.

Scenario:

You are working on completing your tasks and a coworker, friend, family member, etc. shows up and asks you for a "small" favor that requires you to interrupt what you are doing (or requires you to stay late / give up your weekend / etc.) and spend considerable time on completing that "small" favor.

How do you say "NO" without hurting that person's feelings?

1. The **"YES, but..."** technique

"I would love to help you with that...

"That sounds like fun...

"Of course, I'd be glad to....

... **but** right now I'm in the middle of a project that I must finish today."

Then you reach for your planner (or not) and say "Would Thursday afternoon be a good time for me to help you with that?"

You can use endless variations of the above method; and if the person really needs your help, then they'll wait till you have the time for it. Chances are, however, that most people will take care of whatever they need without your involvement. Fact is, people are drawn to your kind and helpful attitude, and some can easily get "addicted" to requesting your help for all kinds of trivial (or not so trivial) matters.

2. The **"not an expert"** technique

"I'd love to help you with that, but I'm not very good at...(whatever the task implies)" or... "... I really don't think I'm the right person to help you with this."

Of course, you can use this technique only if there's at least a bit of truth behind it.

3. The **"I already have plans"** technique

"I'd really love to go / I'd really love to help you, but (this sounds like a time-consuming project and) I already have plans for this afternoon/week-end/etc. If you really need my help, we can try to squeeze it in next week sometimes"

4. The **"What's the priority?"** technique
   If your boss (or spouse, etc.) wants to dump a new task on you, while you already work on some time-consuming task(s)...
   "I'm already working on [...], which you've requested I submit before the end of the day. Which one has a higher priority?"

5. The **"I'd rather not..."** technique
   "I'd love to help you, but with the hectic schedule I have these days, I'd probably do a sloppy job at it. I'd rather not do it than mess it up."

6. The **"Let me get back to you on that"** technique
   "Let me check my planner and I'll get back to you on that before the end of the day"
   If you are a busy "bee," chances are that your schedule is busier than you'd like to; so get back to the person and be honest. Let them know that your schedule is really full; but if they can't find anyone, you'd be glad to help on "next Friday afternoon."

7. The **"Just say 'NO'"** technique
   "Sorry, I can't right now – I'm in the middle of [...] something and I have this pile to finish before the end of the day/week..."

It is ok to say "NO" once in a while. Sometimes you are just so busy with ongoing projects that it'd be really silly to take on some more tasks. And if someone can't understand that, they deserve to have their feelings hurt; that way they won't bother you any soon. Besides, practicing saying a firm "NO," shows assertiveness and self-confidence.

Of course, make sure you don't "over-practice" saying "NO." People love you because you are helpful and kind. Don't spoil your image by saying "no" to everything; but don't let others take advantage of you either. Keep things in balance by saying "NO" (in one of the above ways or their variations) whenever you can't comfortably accommodate others' requests, or when helping others would cut into your personal/family time.

REMEMBER! Whenever you say "NO" in any of the above forms, stay calm and project confidence; and most importantly, do not lie in order to refuse someone's request – you don't want to tarnish your reputation...

APPENDIX E

Become a DISC
Trainer/Facilitator/Consultant/Coach

Provide companies with DISC training or consulting; or provide one-on-one or group coaching utilizing DISC concepts.

Visit **www.egsebastian.com/products_by_application** to see Inscape's DiSC® [1] (and other) assessments in different applications (Change Management, Coaching, Customer Service, Sales, Diversity, Leadership, Management Development, Teams, and Time Management).

Get started in a matter of days with the Facilitator Kit of your choice!

Each facilitator kit includes:

- Scripted modules that can be used as stand-alone workshops or can be combined into half-day or full-day seminars
- Professionally designed, customizable PowerPoint slides
- Professional designed and customizable handouts for creating participant manuals
- Professional training DVD with individually selectable segments
(DVD to be used during presentation, as well as to train the trainer)

See complete details and view sample videos at

http://egsebastian.com/facilitator_kits

For more information, please call Toll Free 877 379-3793!

Or contact us by eMail at support@egSebastian.com

---

[1] DiSC® with lower case "I" is an Inscape Publishing, Inc trademark

Communication Skills Magic

How to Understand and Motivate Your Employees Most Effectively

180-Minutes 2-CD Set with Workbook

With instant mp3 download available at no extra cost!

In this program you will learn:
o How to easily recognize each behavioral style in your environment
o How to communicate most effectively with each style
o How to prevent conflict with each style
o How to deal with conflict with each style
o How to create an environment that's most inductive for higher productivity for each style
o How to motivate each style
o How to coach each style towards higher performance

Price: $47.00 + Shipping and Handling
(Allow 7 to 10 days for delivery)

For more info or to order,
Please visit www.egSebastian.com/cdMot
or call Toll Free 877 379-3793

Communication Skills Magic

Improve Your Relationship with Your Child and Spouse (or Significant Other)
120-Minutes CD with Workbook

With instant mp3 download available at no extra cost!

How would it impact your life at the present moment if you could dramatically improve your relationships with your loved ones? How much conflict and stress would be eliminated from your days...? How much more joyful moments could you share with those you love?

In this program you will learn:
- better understand your own personality and communication style
- easily recognize the (four) personality and communication style of your loved ones
- learn strategies on how to flex your communication style in order to communicate with your loved ones more effectively based on their natural communication and behavioral tendencies
- explore what naturally motivates the personality style of your loved ones
- learn simple strategies on how to prevent conflict with your loved ones
- find out how to deal with conflict with each style
- become a better parent or spouse by becoming a masterful communicator

Price: $37.00 + Shipping and Handling
(Allow 7 to 10 days for delivery)

For more info or to order,
Please visit www.egSebastian.com/cdFam
or call Toll Free 877 379-3793

Order Form

Please send me the following product (s):

	Price	Quantity	Total

Communication Skills Magic (soft cover) $17.95   _____

_____

(For volume discount – above 10 copies – please see Appendix C)

Communication Skills Magic – How to
Understand and Motivate Your Employees
Most Effectively (90-min. Audio CD) $27.00   _____

Communication Skills Magic
– Improve Your Relationship with Your
Child and Spouse or Significant Other
(120-min. Audio CD) $37.00   _____

Shipping & Handling: **$5.50**   _____
(Buying more than one product?
Please add $1.00 for every additional item)   _____

International Shipping: $7.50   _____
(Please add $3.50 for every additional item)

Payment ____ Check ____ Credit Card:

____ Visa ____ Master Card ____ PayPal (use links on previous pages)

Name on Card:_____

Card Number:_____ Exp. Date: _____

Fax Orders on this Form to: 843 470-9096 (Attn: E.G. Performance Solutions)

TOLL FREE Telephone Orders: 877 379 3793 International: 843 379-3793

Email Orders to: support@egSebastian.com

Send **Postal Orders** to: E.G. Performance Solutions, 330 Robert Smalls Pkwy,

Ste 24, Beaufort, SC 29906

To <u>learn more about Inscape learning tools and facilitator kits</u>, please
visit **http://egsebastian.com/facilitator_kits**,
or call TOLL FREE 877 379-3793 for more information.

**Sign up for FREE Online Video Training and
Tutorials
at www.egSebastian.com/FREE_Training**

More Resources from E.G. Sebastian:

www.disc411.com
www.discChat.com
www.egSebastian.com
www.discSalesStyles.com
www.discBuyingStyles.com
www.iReadBodyLanguage.com
www.BecomeAdiscTrainer.com
www.CommunicationSkillsMagic.com

Made in the USA
Lexington, KY
27 July 2015